Go-Givers in a Go-Getter World

Go-Givers
in a
Go-Getter
World

Paul W. Powell

BROADMAN PRESS
Nashville, Tennessee

© Copyright 1986 • Broadman Press
All Rights Reserved
4225-46

ISBN: 0-8054-2546-2
Dewey Decimal Classification: 254
Subject Headings: CHURCH GROWTH
Library of Congress Catalog Number: 86-17105

Printed in the United States of America

Unless otherwise stated, all Scripture quotations are from the King James Version of the Bible.

Scripture quotations marked RSV are from the Revised Standard Version of the Bible, copyrighted 1946, 1952, © 1971, 1973.

Scripture quotations marked NASB are from the *New American Standard Bible.* Copyright © The Lockman Foundation, 1960, 1962, 1963, 1968, 1971, 1972, 1973, 1975, 1977. Used by permission.

Scripture quotations marked NEB are from *The New English Bible.* Copyright © The Delegates of the Oxford University Press and the Syndics of the Cambridge University Press, 1961, 1970. Reprinted by permission.

Library of Congress Cataloging-in-Publication Data

Powell, Paul W.
  Go-givers in a go-getter world.

  1. Church growth.   2. Evangelistic work.   I. Title.
BV652.25.P67 1986   254'.5   86-17105
ISBN 0-8054-2546-2

To Dennis Parrott.
When you read Chapter 9,
you will know why.

Contents

Contents

Introduction

Christians of today have the most creative collection of tools by which to evangelize the world of any generation in history: satellite broadcasting, transistor radios, massive evangelistic crusades, and the increasing use of all kinds of media. And we have a host of parachurch organizations with catchy slogans like "World evangelization in our generation" to match our methods.

But where is the local church in all of this strategizing? Not nearly enough is being spoken and written about its role in winning our world to Christ.

It is my conviction that the local church must be at the core of world evangelization. Any effective strategy for winning our generation to Christ must focus on the building of strong and vital churches that will function as salt and light in the world.

The message of the gospel is not an abstraction. Christ becomes known in the best sense as He is incarnated in His church and people. When the church is healthy and vital, it is the most effective means of winning people to Christ.

My plea in this book is simple: it is time to refocus our thinking on the building of evangelistic churches that can reach and keep converts. This should be the central part of our evangelistic strategy.

To do this, churches and leaders alike must awaken out of their lethargy and be willing to take risks for the cause of

Christ. The ministry of preaching, teaching, and witnessing must be shared by the whole church. The concept of servant-hood and ministry to the needs of people must be recaptured. We must look again at what we mean by "a shared ministry." We must begin to use the spiritual gifts of our members and challenge them to perform their role in the body of Christ.

To build this type of evangelistic church is no easy undertak-ing. It will require a shift in our priorities, and we may not see immediate results. But I am convinced that this is the stuff from which world evangelization is made.

I offer this book as an encouragement to that end.

1
Risktakers/Caretakers/ Undertakers

Dr. Bob Cox, a deacon in our church and dean of the Department of Education at the University of Texas in Tyler, recently told me that most institutions and movements eventually go through three stages. They begin as risktakers, then they grow to be caretakers, and eventually they end up as undertakers.

Churches are no exception.

Many churches are in the undertaker's stage of existence: they are dead and don't know it. To be in their services is like attending the annual board meeting of a perpetual-care cemetery. Like the church at Sardis, they are living on their past reputations. Sardis had a glorious past but a poor present performance (see Rev. 3:1).

Some years ago a best-selling novel began, "The courthouse clock struck twelve, and the church on the corner was giving up its dead." That characterizes many churches today.

Long before churches are undertakers, they become caretakers. Their attitude is: "We are big enough, we have built enough, we have borrowed enough." Like the church at Laodicea (see Rev. 3:16), they are "lukewarm" and "at ease in Zion." They are often referred to as "sleeping giants"—with the emphasis on *sleeping*.

Some churches climb to the top and then settle down so hard they flatten out. They become big and then start to rest on their laurels. They reach a certain point, and then they merely settle back and stop trying. Watch out for the comfortable rut! Comfort comes as a guest, lingers to become a host, and stays to enslave us.

Churches ought to be risktakers. We need to be like Paul and Barnabas, the first missionaries of the church in Antioch who were described as "men that have hazarded their lives for the name of our Lord Jesus Christ" (Acts 15:26). The word *hazarded* is a gambling term that means "to wager, to take a risk, to lay something on the line."

These early disciples were so convinced of human lostness, the truthfulness of the gospel, and the necessity of missions and evangelism that they risked both life and limb to carry the old story into new places. There was nothing complacent about them. They were obsessed and possessed by the Master's mandate to carry the gospel to all persons everywhere. To this end they spent and were spent, and they considered the price cheap compared to the glory that awaited them. They were people on a bold mission—consumed and committed.

Churches today must be risktakers in that same sense. The greatest achievements in the history of the church and of missions have been the outcome of leaders in touch with God, leaders who took courageous, carefully calculated risks.

One of my military heroes, General George Patton, in a speech to his troops, declared, "There is one thing I want you to remember. I don't want to get any messages saying we are holding our position. We are advancing constantly. We are not interested in holding anything except the enemy."

His motto was: "Always take the offensive. Never dig in!"

Jesus obviously expected His church to assume that kind of aggressive offensive, for He stated to His apostles, "Upon this rock I will build my church; and the gates of hell shall not prevail against it" (Matt. 16:18).

In ancient times the gates of cities were for defensive purposes. Cities were built with huge walls around them and gates that could be closed at night or in times of war. In order to conquer the city, an invading army would have to storm the walls and knock down the gates. Jesus visualized His church as on the offensive, storming the very gates of hell. And He predicted that hell could not withstand the onslaught of His militant church.

But too many churches today have developed a maintenance mentality. They have dug in and are content to hold onto what they have, rather than gearing up and launching out. Most of their plans are made for the convenience of their members, rather than for the advancement of God's kingdom. In many instances today, the church is so organized that she is muscle-bound, so prosperous that she is fat and out of breath.

What is the mission of the church? What is our calling? Jesus forever settled that when He commissioned, "Go ye therefore, and teach all nations, baptizing them in the name of the Father, and of the Son, and of the Holy Ghost: Teaching them to observe all things whatsoever I have commanded you: and, lo, I am with you alway, even unto the end of the world" (Matt. 28:19-20).

Our mission is the Great Commission. Our goal is not necessarily to build big churches. That would be self-seeking and unworthy of the gospel. Our goal is to reap the maximum yield from our field. It is to do the best we can with what we have, where we are, for Jesus' sake today.

We are to busy ourselves at winning, baptizing, and teaching people and to stay constantly at it until Jesus comes again or calls time on us. To fulfill our mission, we must do three things: we must bring people in, we must build them up, and we must send them out.

Bring Them in

An article from the weekly paper of one of our largest and most prestigious churches in America stated recently that a remarkable happening occurred in their staff planning retreat last year. "For the first time in anyone's memory there was complete, one hundred percent unity concerning where the priorities should be placed in every area of our church life—EVANGELISM!"

To me, the remarkable matter is not that their staff agreed evangelism was their first priority. It is that anyone would ever have suggested anything else. For a church to decide to give priority to evangelism is like a hospital giving priority to health care, a railroad giving priority to transportation, or AT & T giving priority to communications. What else could it be? That is our mission also.

Our first responsibility is always to introduce the lost to Christ. When I was a boy, we used to sing:

> Hark! 'Tis the Shepherd's voice I hear,
>   Out in the desert dark and drear,
> Calling the sheep who've gone astray
>   Far from the Shepherd's fold away.

> Bring them in, bring them in,
>   Bring them in from the fields of sin;
> Bring them in, bring them in,
>   Bring the wandering ones to Jesus.

I've noticed we don't sing that hymn much anymore. Maybe we quit singing it because we first quit doing it.

In 1848, John Geddie, a Canadian Presbyterian missionary, went to the New Hebrides Islands in the South Pacific to work. He was in constant peril of his life but won the confidence of the dangerous cannibals. He developed an alphabet and translated the New Testament into their dialect and, also many hymns of the church. One by one he taught them, and they gave up their heathen gods and superstitions. Several churches were built. By 1854 more than half of the four thousand people on that island had become Christians. The natives then began to go to other islands with the gospel.

When John Geddie died, a marble slab bearing this inscription was placed on his grave:

> When he came here,
>   There were no Christians;
> When he went away,
>   There were no heathen.

That is our first duty: to win the lost, to bring them in.

Build Them Up

After we have brought them in, we must then build them up. We must teach them to obey all the things that Jesus commanded us. Conversion is a germinal, not a terminal, experience. New life in Christ is like a tender plant. It must be cultivated and cared for to grow to its full potential.

Many evangelists and pastors have been asked: "Will these new converts thrive?" We sometime reply that the same question could just as sensibly be asked of newborn infants in a maternity ward. "The answer is 'No, they will not thrive—not unless for a long time they are cared for, nurtured, and helped to grow.' "

When a baby is born, what do we do with it? Do we put it in a refrigerator? No! That's a good place for a head of lettuce, a bottle of milk, or a pound of bologna, but it is a poor place for a baby. We can't put new converts—"babes in Christ"— into refrigerator churches either. They need to be in an incubator church in order to thrive spiritually.

The church is to be both obstetrician and pediatrician. We are to help people be born again through faith in the Lord Jesus, and then help them to grow to full maturity in Christ.

How do new converts grow? How are they built up? Peter

wrote that like newborn babes we should desire the "pure milk" of God's Word in order to grow thereby (1 Pet. 2:2, NASB).

Jesus taught us that mankind does not live by bread alone "but by every word that proceedeth out of the mouth of God" (Matt. 4:4).

There is a spiritual part of us that cannot be nourished or satisfied with meat and potatoes alone. It requires regular feeding upon the Word of God to sustain us.

It is a part of the church's mission to provide warm and loving fellowship where the Word of God is taught and where opportunities for service are provided, so new Christians can grow to maturity in the Lord.

The apostle Paul prayed that the church at Ephesus might be "strengthened with might by his Spirit in the inner man" (Eph. 3:16). Satan, through temptations and trials, exerts tremendous pressure on believers in order to crush their faith. After we have brought people in, we must then build them up so they will have inner braces for these outer pressures of life.

Send Them Out

After we have brought them in and built them up, we must then send them back out into the world to witness and to work for Christ. It is not enough merely to ring church bells, we must also ring doorbells. We must see the church, not as a place of evangelism, but as the base of evangelism. It is a launching pad from which witnessing saints go out to tell the world about Christ.

C. E. Autrey was right in urging us to give the church a chance to breathe by going outside. Remember, it is the Sermon on the Mount, not the sermon in the cathedral, that Jesus preached and which has changed the world.

The Lord never intended that worldlings should come to the church to find Christ. He intended that the church should be in the world sharing Christ.

In the parable of the great supper, the master who represents

God sent his servants out three different times to invite people to the supper. The third time he told them to go and "compel" people to come. The word *compel* is an exceedingly strong word. It literally means "to necessitate." Those servants would be going to people who ordinarily would feel unworthy, unwanted, and unwelcome. The master told them that they must impress upon these people that they were wanted, welcome, and worthy.

That is also our mission. As those servants went out again and again, so we must go out repeatedly. As they went everywhere, so we must go everywhere—to crowded cities, to affluent suburbs, to sleepy hamlets, and down quiet country roads. And as they went with a sense of urgency, so we must also go in urgency.

A man returned to his hometown after being gone for many years. As he looked around at familiar faces and places, he noticed that the old church where he had once worshiped was no longer there. He asked the man who had run the service station since he was a child, "Whatever happened to that old church and the glory it once had?"

The attendant asked him, "Are you going to be driving around town some more today?" He replied, "Yes."

Then the attendant said, "If you will drive up the hill over there where the church used to be, you will see a sign. Read it carefully for it will tell you what happened to that old church and the glory that it once had."

Later that evening the man started up the hill. It was getting dark, so he slowed down to catch the message written on the sign. As his headlights focused on it the motorist read these words: "Drive Carefully: Children at Play."

If we are going to fulfill our mission today, we cannot be playing at the task. We must become militant and take the offensive at bringing people in, building them up, and sending them out. And we must do it at all costs, regardless of the risks. That is the only way to grow an evangelistic church.

2
Growth with Integrity

General Patton, in the movie about his life, spoke of Britain's Field Marshal Montgomery, "Montgomery seems to be more concerned about not losing a battle than winning one." That same attitude characterizes many churches and many Christian leaders today: they are more concerned about not losing than winning. They merely "want to hold their own."

Robert Louis Stevenson described this attitude of safety, security, and prudence as "that dismal fungus." Like a cancer in the body, it will eventually consume us if we do not rid ourselves of it. As followers of Christ, we must never be content to maintain the status quo.

Jesus assigned us our mission in Luke 19:13 with, "Occupy till I come." The last week of Jesus' life was approaching. As He and His disciples neared the city of Jerusalem, their Messianic hopes reached a fevered pitch. The disciples still thought, though He had repeatedly explained otherwise, that He would establish an earthly kingdom and rule the world from Jerusalem.

To clear up their misconceptions once and for all, Jesus presented the parable of the pounds: the story of a wealthy businessman who planned a brief trip into a far country. The man represented Jesus Himself. In preparation for his journey the man called in ten of his servants and gave to each of them a sum of money called a pound. These servants represented His disciples, and the pounds symbolized His work, His business, His kingdom.

His final instruction to them was, "Occupy till I come." Those words forever settled the mission of God's people. To occupy does not mean to "sit on" or to "hold on" but to "get on" with His work. It literally implies "to be busy about." The Lord expects us to be busy about His business until He comes again. This is forever and always the work of the church: God's people.

And we are to be aggressive in that work. When Jesus spoke of His church, "The gates of hell shall not prevail against it" (Matt. 16:18), He suggested that His church was to be militantly aggressive. We are to be on the offensive without being offensive.

In this parable, the faithfulness of three of the ten servants is evaluated. The first servant increased his master's money by ten times and was duly rewarded upon the master's return. The second servant multiplied his five times, and he too was duly rewarded when his master returned.

The third servant, however, was a caretaker, not a risktaker. He had a maintenance mentality; he "played it safe." So he hid his pound until his master returned. When he reported no profit, the master was displeased and took all the servant had from him, and gave it to those servants who had been faithful. The third servant was left with absolutely no reward.

It is interesting that the longest speech in this parable is from the man who did nothing as he tried to justify his failure. He spoke forty words for his alibi—to report that he had done nothing.

Those who did their duty and were faithful to their master's trust required only seven words to give their progress report. Many people are going to be stammering for words, filibustering on judgment day as they try to explain why they did nothing. And those who have done the least will talk the most!

Apparently, the third servant thought it was good that he had returned the pound with no loss. The master called him wicked because the servant returned it with no gain. Can the Scriptures be clearer? It is not enough *not to lose*. We are expected to *win*.

At the outset of this parable Jesus declared that we are to busy ourselves about His work until He comes again. What was His basic work? He spelled it out just three verses prior to this parable. "For the Son of man is come to seek and to save that which was lost" (Luke 19:10).

We are to give ourselves in seeking the lost. Then Jesus does the saving. We are to busy ourselves at increasing His kingdom.

How do we do this? How do we build an evangelistic church? How do we go about winning and holding members? I want to offer six suggestions.

It Will Cost You Your Life

The first step in growing an evangelistic church is to make a commitment to growth. For the past twelve years I've had the privilege of pastoring a growing, evangelistic church. Our city is a small East Texas community with a population of seventy-five thousand people. It has experienced a healthy 30 percent growth over the past ten years. During that same period of time, our average Sunday School attendance has increased 300 percent: from an average of seven hundred to over twenty-three hundred per Sunday. And the growth in the other areas of our church life has been comparable.

When people hear about our growth, they sometimes comment, "You just happened to be in the right place at the right time." I would be the last person to discount the importance of being at the right place at the right time. It does help. One can't grow a church in the Sahara Desert. We must be where people are. However, there have been other churches at the same place during the same period of time that have not grown. So there must be more to it than that.

An illustration in contrast will show what I am talking about. I know of two churches in a thriving city that have many factors in common. In addition to being in the same town, the two churches are nearly the same age. One is twenty-eight years old, and the other is twenty-nine. Both are located in the same part of their city. One is located directly across the street from one end of a small shopping center, and the other right across the street from the opposite end of that same shopping center. And they both have access to the same Bible: the King James Version, red-letter edition! That's the only kind we use in East Texas. But that is where the similarities end.

While one has grown to a membership of over five thousand, the other has only three-hundred members. While one has an average Sunday School attendance of over twenty-one hundred, the other church averages less than one hundred. While one had total receipts of three million dollars last year, the other received less than a hundred-thousand dollars. And, finally, while one had over six-hundred additions to its fellowship last year, the other had only twenty-nine additions.

Now, how do we account for this wide difference, seeing that both churches are in the same place at the same time with the same opportunity? What makes the difference? It is obviously more than being in the right place at the right time.

I believe that the explanation is commitment. One church has, through the years, had a commitment to growth; the other has not. One has been committed to carrying out the Great Commission, to winning the lost, to evangelizing its community. The other has not. That is the difference.

Such a commitment to growth on the part of the pastor and the people is, I believe, the single most important factor in growing an evangelistic church. I think it is more important than its theological positions; after all, Robert Schuller of the

Garden Grove Community Church in California has built a growing church on "possibility thinking." It is more important than location or accessibility, for W. A. Criswell, First Baptist Church, Dallas, Texas, has built a growing church in the heart of a throbbing metropolis. And it is more important than being in the Bible Belt, for Jack Hyles, First Baptist Church, Hammond, Indiana, has built a growing church in a Northern industrial area.

Commitment is the key. At our church we make a great commotion over the Great Commission. That is the primary reason why we have grown.

The Buck Stops Here

The second step in growing an evangelistic church is dynamic leadership. Will Rogers once mused that the history of America will be written in three phases: the passing of the Indian, the passing of the buffalo, and the passing of the buck!

We might as well face it: the buck stops with leadership. One cannot grow an evangelistic church without strong, dynamic leadership. Churches almost never rise above their leaders. What does it require to be a dynamic leader? What is involved in leadership? I will elaborate in more detail in the next chapter, but for the time being let me point to three ideas: you must see what needs to be done, develop a plan for doing it, and then enlist and motivate others to help you do it.

Real leadership begins with vision: seeing what needs to be done. Do not assume that there is an abundance of this. John Ruskin opined, "The greatest thing a human soul ever does in this world is to see something and to tell what he saw in a plain way. Hundreds of people can talk for one who can think, but thousands can think for one who can see."

Leadership requires that we develop a plan for doing what needs to be done. It was facetiously asked, "How do you eat an elephant?" The answer came back, "One bite at a time!" Leaders are people who can analyze a problem and propose a solution that people can sink their teeth into and digest: in bite-sized chunks. Grand ideas need landing gears as well as wings. Leadership involves practicality as well as vision.

Finally, leaders must be able to enlist and inspire other people to join with them in doing what needs to be done. Leaders must be self-motivated. Their push comes inside while most other people must be pushed from outside.

Let me illustrate. Last year we entered into our third major building program in succession. Our plans were to finance two construction projects at once totaling two-and-a-half million dollars. The first would be an enlargement of our sanctuary to double its seating capacity. The second would be to build a three-story adult education building. We would begin with the sanctuary enlargement, and when it was completed, we would start the educational building. The two-and-a-half-million dollars was pledged to be paid over a three-year period.

As we neared the completion of the sanctuary, I could see that we were going to be within a hundred-thousand dollars of having the project completely paid for, and there was a possibility of moving into it debt free. So I wrote ninety-nine men and asked them to join me in giving one thousand dollars extra to pay off this debt on or before the date of dedication. Remember now, one year before, we had pledged two-and-a-half-million dollars, and these men had been paying on their pledges all along. We were also in the midst of a recession.

In addition to those ninety-nine letters, I asked every child under twelve years of age to give at least one dollar to the building fund on dedication day. I made it clear that I did not want their parents to give them the money. I wanted them to work for it and earn it, so it would have special meaning to them. Then I asked every teenager to give at least five dollars and all adults to give as much as they possibly could.

In a matter of a few days I began receiving replies from those letters telling of God's working in the lives of our people. One of the most interesting came from Ben Lester, a pilot with Delta Airlines.

Ben testified that when he received my letter, he talked it over with his wife, Marsha, but they did not have the thousand dollars at the time and did not know where they could find it. He wrote that he and Marsha usually prayed over such matters, but this time they did not even do that because they saw no possibility of responding. As Ben went to bed that night he kept thinking about the letter. The next morning as he headed to work it was still on his mind. Ben was not so much praying about it as merely thinking about it. When he arrived at work the next day, there were two envelopes in his mailbox. He opened the first to find a reimbursement check from his hospitalization insurance company. He had several medical expenses that year, paid those out of his own pocket, and then filed a claim with his insurance company. It usually took about two months for the company to respond. This time they had answered in only two weeks. The check was for $855. Then Ben opened the other envelope. The insurance company had inadvertently sent a payment check to a doctor Ben had already paid. So when the doctor received the insurance company's check, he simply endorsed it and sent it on to Ben. The check was for $150.

You can readily see that Ben now had $1005 that he had not expected to receive. When Ben went home that night, he told Marsha about the two checks, and she exclaimed, "That's God's money. Let's give it to the church." Then Ben called his three boys in to let them share in the decision. He asked them what they thought the family should do. One of them replied, "Let's give it to the church." Another hollered, "Let's spend it!"

Letter after letter came back with similar testimonies of how marvelously God provided money for them to give. When dedication day came, our people gave $255,000, and we entered the building debt free.

That story has all the components of leadership I am talking about: seeing what needs to be done; developing a plan for doing it; and enlisting others to join in achieving it.

The Church Is for Rats

The third factor in growing an evangelistic church is to build a warm and loving fellowship.

Growing evangelistic churches are happy places where people like to be. They cultivate a warm family atmosphere where there are no walls. The spirit of love embraces everyone who walks in the door. The people seem eager to bear one another's burdens. Members like to be there and want others to come also. They are places where all people are loved, accepted, and helped.

Several years ago a lady wrote Ann Landers a scorching letter. Her daughter had recently gone through a divorce, and the mother had suggested that the daughter begin attending church where she might meet a nice man. The daughter did as the mother suggested and did meet a man who came home with her for supper one night. In fact, he came home with her for supper every night for six weeks in a row! Then the mother said, "We found out that the rat was married and was still living at home with his wife and children." Then she said, "The church is for rats!"

When I read that, I thought: *Lady, if you only knew my church. The church is not only for rats, it is for skunks and for snakes-in-the-grass, for donkeys, and for turkeys.*

While we don't want to turn the Lord's sheepfold into a zoo, we are under no illusions about ourselves. We know that the church is an assembly line whose finished product is delivered in heaven. We testify that we are sinners who have been saved by grace, and we welcome other sinners also. People, no matter who they are, can come and feel comfortable with us.

If we are going to have growing, evangelistic churches, we must melt down some of the archness and starchness and join the human race. We can't pretend we are better than we are or worse than we are. We must relax, be ourselves, and let others do the same. In a loving and accepting atmosphere God can do His greatest work of evangelism and growth.

But even this comes back to leadership. As Vance Havner put it, "Show me a church that is as cold as an iceberg, and I'll show you a church that has a polar bear in its pulpit."

The Main Thing

Fourth, to grow an evangelistic church. We need to magnify and mobilize the Sunday School. I once read a slogan that went, "The main thing is to keep the main thing the main thing." That's not double talk. It speaks of priorities. Everything can't be first in your life or in your church. So you must keep the main thing the main thing. What is the main thing? In order to reach people, I believe it is Sunday School.

Sunday School is not merely another organization of the church. It is the church organized and functioning to carry out the Great Commission.

The Sunday School is the place where the Bible is taught, where a loving spirit is caught, and where the lost are sought. That makes it the main thing at our place.

People want and need to be taught the Bible. Dr. Robert Gehring, a physician, shared his testimony in our church recently. He confessed that in seeking victory over alcoholism and drug addiction, "I spent twenty-two thousand dollars on shrinks and found my help in a ten-dollar Bible." Listen! When we find a Bible that's falling apart, it usually belongs to a person who isn't.

People want and need to be a part of a caring and sharing

fellowship. I once read a slogan on a church bulletin: "Why join a church when you can join a family?" Sunday School helps to make the church a family where people can feel at home and make friends.

And Sunday School is the best way to reach the lost and unenlisted for Christ and His church.

A Multiple-Option Program

John Naisbitt, in his book *Megatrends,* points out that we are shifting from an either/or to a multiple-option society. We are seeing the emerging of what he calls the "Baskin-Robbins Society." Baskin-Robbins, you know, is an ice-cream company that features thirty-one flavors of ice cream.

When I was a boy, we had only three flavors of ice cream: chocolate, vanilla, and strawberry. Who could ever want more than that? But today Baskin-Robbins and other ice cream vendors offer more choices than I can remember.

If you want to buy a car in the United States, there are over seven-hundred-and-fifty-two models to choose from, and that doesn't include all the various color options. There is a store in New York City that sells twenty-five hundred different kinds of lightbulbs!

Life was once so simple. If I wanted a soft drink when I was a boy, there was only one kind and one size of each brand. Today there are all sizes and all kinds: regular, sugar-free, caffeine-free, both sugar-free and caffeine-free, with or without a popular artificial sweetener. If the manufacturers keep taking ingredients out of soft drinks, we will soon be buying only the can.

The time was when, if you wanted to watch television, you had only three network choices. But today there are all-news networks, all-sports networks, all-Spanish networks, all-black networks, all-religious networks, all-music networks, and all-children's networks. And right now some have as many as one-hundred channels from which to choose programs.

It appears that the next generation will have eyes the size of saucers and brains the size of a split pea.

In a multiple-option society, the church that offers only preaching, singing, and Sunday School is like an Amish family trying to drive a horse and buggy down the Pennsylvania Turnpike. It will be an oddity that will soon be passed by. Our churches must think, dream, and innovate. "Business as usual" won't get the job done.

Recently, one of my assistants told me that we had twenty-five different outreach ministries in our church. One of the most recent is a ministry to alcoholics. We offer a support group to people who have either had, or are now having problems with alcohol or drugs, or who have family members with these problems. I announced the beginning of this group one Sunday morning, and twelve people showed up for a Tuesday morning breakfast. The group has been growing ever since.

The next Sunday after I made that announcement, a young nurse joined our church. She exulted, "I want to be a part of a church that cares about people like that." A young salesman came to talk with me about his father's drinking problem. The end result was: we not only helped his dad, but that young man himself was reached for Christ. People think of our church as being in touch with reality and caring about their needs. That's why many of them come.

When a deacon friend of mine, Blake Gillen, invites people to church, he says to them, "Come visit our church. We'll treat you so many ways you are bound to like one of them." The growing, evangelistic churches of today are those that offer people such a multiple ministry.

You've Got to Fight for Them

The final step in growing an evangelistic church is hard work. One can't enjoy the luxury of success without the price of sacrifice.

A man with two swollen and discolored eyes went into a bar, "Boy, they are beauties," said the bartender. "Who gave them to you?" "They don't give these away," replied the man. "You have to fight for them!"

It is the same with growing an evangelistic church. It is never a gift. It takes hard work. You've got to fight to make it so.

I was in Loveland, Colorado, several years ago for a church growth seminar. When I checked into the motel, a sign over the desk captured my attention. It read, "There ain't hardly no business here that ain't been went after."

That's not the best English, but if the purpose of language is to communicate, it does the job. That's the way it is at our church. We have averaged over eleven additions per Sunday for the past thirteen years. But they haven't come easily or automatically.

Recently, I took a seventh grader, Matt Ellis, visiting with me. Matt was working on his "God and Country Award" for the Boy Scouts, and participation in church visitation was one of his projects.

On our way home I asked Matt, "How did you like visiting?" He answered, "Just fine. Now, I understand why Green Acres has grown so big. We get after them."

Matt was exactly right. They come in because we go out. It is with us as it is with the motel: "There ain't hardly no people joined here that ain't been went after."

Most church members today have been sitting so long they have ingrown shirttails. If our churches are going to grow, we must declare war on laziness and indifference. We must give ourselves with new enthusiasm and tireless labor to the work of God. There are entirely too many people like the former staff member of mine that I talked to last week. When I asked him how he was doing, he replied, "Great! I've got a pastor who doesn't do anything, and I'm helping him." There are a lot of people in our churches today who aren't doing anything, and there are lots more helping them.

There are no shortcuts to growing an evangelistic church. And laboring for God can be exhausting. But I keep remembering the statement of Winston Churchill, "Most of the significant contributions that have been made to society have been made by people who were tired."

We are people on a mission. We have little time to sit around and enjoy the scenery. There will be time enough for that when we all get to heaven. So until then, we must be about our Master's business. We must occupy until He comes.

3
No Place
for Ministerial Midgets

James Reston, a columnist for *The New York Times,* several years ago gave an evaluation of the small caliber of men that he thought occupied governors' chairs in the various states at that time. He said, "Maybe the states can go on handling bigger and bigger problems with smaller and smaller men, but it is risky business . . . most state capitals are over their heads in problems and up to their knees in midgets."

It takes strong and dynamic leaders to grow the kind of evangelistic church that wins and keeps converts. It can't be done with ministerial midgets. So wherever there is a growing evangelistic church, you will find people who realize the importance of leadership and pay the price to give it.

Before we proceed any further, perhaps we need to pause and define leadership. In the simplest terms, leadership is influence. It is the ability of one person to influence others. One can lead others only to the extent that he can influence them to follow his lead. That fact is supported by definitions of leadership by persons who have themselves wielded great influence.

Lord Montgomery defined leadership as "the capacity and will to rally men and women to a common purpose, and the character which inspires confidence."

Fleet Admiral Nimitz of World War II declared, "Leadership may be defined as that quality in a person that inspires sufficient confidence in his subordinates as to be willing to accept his views and carry out his commands."

And John R. Mott, a world leader in Christian missions, gave as his definition, "A leader is one who knows the road, who can keep ahead, and who pulls others after him."

Leaders must view clearly the goal to be reached, plan imaginative strategy and tactics by which it can be attained, and then convince others to join with them in pursuit of it.

Not every Christian is called to or qualified for a position of major leadership, but all are leaders to the extent that they influence others. All of us can, if we will, increase our leadership potential. All Christians are under obligation to be the best they can be for God. If your leadership potential can be improved, you must do it.

Paul identified leadership as one of the gifts of the Spirit and wrote to the church at Rome and to us, "If you are a leader, exert yourself to lead" (Rom. 12:8, NEB). While the gift is from God, polishing, developing, and improving it is up to us, through His enabling power.

In order to improve our leadership, we need to understand those characteristics that make for good leaders. What are the qualities of leadership necessary to grow an evangelistic church? What does it take to be a good leader?

You Have to Think

The first quality of a good leader is vision. Vision is not seeing the invisible. *It is seeing the obvious that other people overlook.* It is seeing what ought to be done and how to do it.

Vision is the result of a mental process that involves praying, dreaming, and thinking. Thinking is the beginning place of leadership, for we are never free to do a thing we can't think of.

You might believe that people who think are commonplace. Not so. They are always in short supply.

Many people seem to suffer from what Ashley Montague, the great Rutgers anthropolgist, called *psychosclerosis.* Psychosclerosis is like arteriosclerosis. Arteriosclerosis is a hardening of the arteries; psychosclerosis is a hardening of the attitude. When that happens, we cease to dream, to see, to think, and we cease to lead.

It was spoken of Charles Cowman, founder of the Oriental Missionary Society, "He was a man of vision. Throughout his life he seemed to see what the crowd did not see, and to see wider and fuller than many of his own day. He was a man of far horizons."

Those who have most powerfully and permanently influenced their generations have always been the "seers": people who have seen more and farther than others. They have been persons who could think faster, clearer, and farther ahead than those around them.

If you aren't by nature a creative thinker, don't despair. You can still improve your spiritual vision. Read books and periodicals by people who are. Subscribe to the church papers of progressive churches to find out what others are doing.

Associate with people of vision. Make friends with Christian leaders who are dreamers and have lunch with them occasionally. They will stimulate you to greater heights.

Leave your environment periodically so you can see your field in a different light. Then pray much, and you will find your horizons being lifted, and your vision sharpened.

And when you dream, dream big! I visited the Smithsonian Institute while in Washington years ago. There is a marvelous exhibit on city and government planning in which this sign was posted: "Make no little plans, for they have no power to stir men's minds." To be a leader you can't afford to stop dreaming or thinking.

Integrity Is the Word

West German Chancellor Helmut Kohl quipped after his election victory, "My strength is that people are ready to buy a used car from me without testing it first." *That kind of integrity is one of the qualities of any good leader.*

To lead people most effectively, your character must be such that when they do not fully believe in your idea or program, they still believe in you enough to follow. That kind of trust is an awesome responsibility, but it is one of the burdens a leader must bear.

It has always been true that the impact of a message or an idea depends on the character of the one who says it. This conviction is as old as Aristotle. Twenty-five hundred years ago he said,

> We believe good men more readily than others. It is not true, as some writers assume in their treatises or rhetoric, that the personal goodness revealed by the speaker contributes nothing to the power of persuasion: on the contrary, his character may almost be called the most effective means of persuasion he possesses.

It is almost staggering to recount how many times the apostle Paul defended his apostleship and his character in the Epistles of the New Testament. Why did Paul do this so vehemently and so often? It was because he knew that without credibility he had no ministry and no leadership.

So be the kind of honest, straightforward, devout, loving person that people can and will believe, and they will follow you.

Born-Again and "Born-Aginers"

Once you have a vision of what needs to be done, you must then have the courage to carry it out. It takes courage because leadership almost always involves risks: the risk of failure and the risk of opposition.

You will always have critics. No person and no idea will please everybody. Opposition is sure to come. As Morris Gary, a layman in my church, commented, "Some people are born-again and others are born-aginers." Leaders must decide what is right and then go forward in spite of fears and opposition.

While every leader faces the fear of criticism from without, one faces an even greater enemy from within—the fear of failure.

One of our chief dangers is that we may be mastered by our fears, take too many precautions in life, and thus never do anything!

The frontiers of the kingdom of God were never advanced by men and women of caution. Considerably more failure is the result of an excess of caution than of bold experimentation with new ideas. Most of us have never been sufficiently daring.

The difference among men and women is not that some are afraid, and others aren't. The difference is that some are not mastered by their fears. I know that is true with me. Whenever we have launched out on some big project, I have always been afraid. Some people may march forward bravely, but I have most often tiptoed forward timidly. But I don't let anybody know it and never tell people my fears. They already have enough of their own.

When struggling with fear, I keep reminding myself that failure is never fatal, and success is never final. I try to remember that progress always involves risk. You can't steal second base and keep your foot on first.

Presidential primary candidate Jesse Jackson helped us keep the fear of failure in perspective when he explained, concerning his decision to climb into the 1984 presidential race, "If you run, you might lose. If you don't run, you are guaranteed to lose." It is far better to dare mighty feats and experience failure than to live in the safety and the security of mediocrity all of our lives.

Mountain climbers have contended that life always becomes more difficult toward the summit—the cold increases; the responsibility increases.

By its very nature, the position of the leader must be difficult and lonely. You must always be ahead of your followers. Though you may be the friendliest of people, you must be prepared to face the loneliness, criticism, and ostracism. It's a part of the price you must pay for leadership.

The Happy Elephant Approach

Henry J. Kaiser years ago was one of the mighty industralists of America. An associate once commented about him, "Henry is like a happy elephant; he smiles and leans against you. After awhile you know that there is nothing left to do but to move in the direction he is pushing."

Christian leaders need that kind of persistence. We must keep smiling because we are working with volunteer help and free-will offerings. We do not lead by executive memo or imperial edict. We are grass roots, not top brass. But we must keep leaning because people are by nature resistant to new ideas and even progress.

Most churches are asleep, and it requires a loud voice and a daring idea to wake them up. Don't be discouraged if you don't succeed at your initial effort. The first response of sleeping people and sleeping churches, when someone tries to arouse them, is usually to push the snooze button on the alarm clock, roll over, and go back to sleep. And sometimes they even growl at you. Don't be disconcerted. After all, there is no way to awaken a sleeping person without disturbing him. Don't give up. Keep shaking the person gently and he will eventually wake up. Churches are the same way.

Calvin Coolidge noted,

Nothing in the world can take the place of persistency. Talent will not; nothing is more common than unsuccessful people with talent. Genius will not; unrewarded genius is almost a proverb. Education will not; the world is full of educated derelicts. Persistence and determination alone are omnipotent.

A sign outside a small church in upstate New York sums it up pretty well: "Failure is the line of least persistence."

Weigh, then Venture

The fifth quality of a good leader is decisiveness. You must be able to make a decision. If you wait until all possible obstacles are overcome, you will never do anything. So, first weigh, then venture. A thing can be analyzed and scrutinized to death. Study the facts, seek the advice of wise friends, pray diligently, and then decide.

A leader cannot afford to ignore the counsel of cautious persons around him. They will often save the leader from unnecessary mistakes. But he must beware of allowing their excess of caution to curb his initiative, if he feels his vision is of God. Nor must the leader allow cautious persons to restrain him from taking daring steps of faith to which God is calling both leader and followers.

You are going to make mistakes. Everybody does. So expect them and go on. That's another one of the price tags of leadership.

For several years, our church has been involved in mission work in Belize, Central America. Without ever having officially voted to do so, we have built several buildings already and are committed to building others. Last year we had plans to build a church building in the capital city of Belmopan. One day Joe Barentine, who heads up our mission church building projects, told me that plans were ready and a contract agreed upon with a Belizian builder to erect the building. The problem was that we had only half of the fifty thousand dollars needed for the building. But the contractor was available to begin work at once, and the rainy season was approaching, so a decision had to be made immediately. We couldn't wait for our next deacons' meeting or the next church conference. That would take too long.

Fred Swank, who for forty-seven years pastored the Sagamore Hill Baptist Church, Fort Worth, Texas, once confided in me, "It is easier to get forgiveness than to get permission." So I told Joe to go ahead with the building. I knew that was risky business, but a decision had to be made. I would take responsibility. We would obtain the money somehow.

December was approaching, so I added an additional $25,000 to our usual Lottie Moon Christmas Offering goal and told our people what we needed to do. Usually, the World Mission Offering appeal in our church goes like it does in yours. I announce it again and again, then we have to go into January before we reach our goal. But an amazing thing happened this year. We not only raised our sixty-thousand-dollar Lottie Moon Christmas Offering goal, we raised an additional forty-five thousand dollars for the church in Belize—twenty thousand dollars more than we needed—and it all came in before the end of December!

I don't recommend that you do what I do. Your personality, your relationship to your people, the size of your congregation, and the tenure of your service all have something to do with that kind of decision making. There was a time when I would not have dared make a decision like that. But I know my people, and they know me. We trust one another. And I generally know what I can safely do or not do.

The size of the church also has much to do with it. It is far easier to rock a rowboat than a battleship. One person can sink a rowboat, but it would take a sizable crew to rock a battleship. I happen to command a battleship, and that makes it easier for me to make those kinds of decisions.

Learn to Eat Crow

Sixth, humility is an important quality in Christian leadership. If you make a mistake, admit it and apologize for it. The most important seven words of a Christian leader are: "I'm sorry; I was wrong; forgive me."

Christian leaders must learn to eat crow. I have eaten crow every way it can be prepared: fried, stewed, baked, barbecued, and even "extra crispy." While I still gag on it, I have never died from it. In fact, I have discovered that my leadership actually flourishes on it. Persons who must always be right, can never be wrong, and must always have their own way are destined to have trouble as Christian leaders. Don't take yourself too seriously. Join the human race. Get rid of the "god complex" that makes you think you should always be right and never make a mistake. Keep a sense of humor and a humble spirit. Learn to laugh, especially at yourself. You can't take the ministry too seriously, but you can take yourself too seriously.

Attitudes and Altitudes

The seventh quality of a good leader is an optimistic, enthusiastic attitude. A pessimist never makes an inspiring leader. Hope and optimism are essential qualities for the servants of God as they battle with the denizens of darkness for human souls.

Some people are whipped before they start. They always look on the dark side and expect the worst to happen.

Many people are like the boy who came home from school and reported to his father, "Dad, I think I failed my arithmetic test today." The father, desiring to teach the boy to be a positive thinker, challenged, "Son, think positively." The boy responded, "All right, Dad, I'm positive I failed my arithmetic test today." They are positively negative.

The pessimist sees a difficulty in every opportunity. The optimist sees an opportunity in every difficulty. The pessimist, always seeing difficulties before possibilities, tends to hold back the person of vision who desires to push ahead. The cautious person has a part to play in helping optimistic leaders to be realistic as well. But you must watch lest your native and now-ingrained caution clips the wings of the leader God intends to soar.

People catch our spirit just like they catch our colds—by getting close to us. So maintain an infectious optimism and a burning enthusiasm. Whatever you do, put your whole heart into it. Show excitement and be energetic, and others will also.

There you have them, the seven qualities of good leadership:

1. Vision
2. Integrity
3. Courage
4. Persistence
5. Decisiveness
6. Humility
7. Optimism

Cultivate these qualities in your life and ministry, and you will become a good leader. If you aren't a successful leader yet, don't despair, and don't give up. I'm persuaded that leaders are developed, not born. And it is oftentimes a long and grueling process.

After leading his Washington Redskins to a Super Bowl Championship in 1983, Joe Gibbs was elected NFL coach of the year. One newspaper called him, "An overnight success twenty years in the making."

Some of us, like Joe Gibbs, are "late bloomers." So keep dreaming, keep growing, and keep working at it. One day it will come.

4
The Power
and Potential for Growth

William Jennings Bryan once ate a piece of watermelon that was so good he wrapped some of the seeds in a napkin and took them home to plant them in his garden. That night he began to think about the power and potential for growth that was in those seeds. So when he reached home, he weighed the seeds and determined that it would take about five thousand of them to weigh one pound. And he estimated that the watermelon weighed about forty pounds. He then applied mathematics to the watermelon.

Months before, someone had planted a little seed in the ground. Under the influence of sunshine and showers, the little seed had taken off its coat and gone to work. The result was that it had multiplied itself about two-hundred thousand times in weight. On the outside it had put on a covering of green, within a rind of white, and within that a core of red meat. Then it had scattered throughout itself hundreds of little seeds, each one capable of doing the same work all over again.

Seeds do have tremendous power and potential for growth. In fact, there is nothing quite so powerful as growth. We have all seen the roots of a tree split concrete pavement, and a weed push its green head through an asphalt parking lot.

Only yesterday, I saw this power of growth in action. I drove by a huge discount store that had closed six months ago. Today its parking lot is literally covered with weeds and grass. Years ago a contractor dug out the soil of that area and replaced it with iron-ore gravel. Then he graded it, watered it, and packed it again and again. He repeated the process until it was as hard as concrete. Then he sprayed it with oil, covered it with four inches of hot asphalt, and packed that solid. Then for sixteen years it was continually pounded by the cars of shoppers. After all of that, one would think that nothing would ever grow there again. But today, weeds and grass are growing on that parking lot everywhere.

The reason is that tiny seeds were in the soil beneath the asphalt, all alone, simply waiting for a chance to poke their heads out into the sunlight. When the cars stopped parking on them long enough, they sprouted and began to grow. And if left alone, in a few years the parking lot will be completely overcome by grass and weeds. Such is the power of a seed.

Jesus likened His church and the kingdom of God to the seed. In Mark 4 He gave us three parables to illustrate this truth: the parables of the sower, the blade, and the mustard seed. A parable is "an earthly story with a heavenly meaning." Jesus often used these simple stories from life to teach us about His kingdom.

The parable of the sower is the story of a farmer who went into his field to plant seeds. In that day, planting was done by the broadcast method. The farmer scattered the seed by hand in front of him as he walked up and down the rows of the field. Obviously, he would not have complete control over where the seeds fell—especially on a windy day. So some of the seeds fell on the hardened pathway that people used as they crossed the field. Others fell on shallow soil, and still others fell among the thorns along the edges of the field. But some fell on the fertile, plowed soil.

The seeds that fell on the trail were soon eaten by the birds. Those that fell on the stony ground grew for a while but soon withered in the heat because there was no depth to the soil. And the seeds that fell among the thorns grew, but the tender plants were eventually choked out by the other vegetation.

However, the seeds that fell on the good soil yielded abundantly: some as much as one-hundred times.

In the parable of the blades, Jesus compared His kingdom to a man who plants seed in the ground and then goes on about the normal activities of his life because the seed grows all by itself, spontaneously.

He doesn't try to make it grow. In fact, he doesn't even understand how it all happens. The seed has life in itself, so a tiny blade appears first, then an ear and, eventually, a full harvest. When the field is ripe, the farmer puts the scythe to work and gathers in the grain.

Finally, Jesus compared the kingdom of God to a mustard seed. The mustard seed was considered one of the smallest in the Eastern world. But when it was planted, it grew into a large bush ten to twelve feet high with branches that shot out in all directions. These branches provided shelter for birds.

Jesus taught these three parables to show us how the kingdom of God grows, the extent of growth we should expect from it, and our part in the growth process.

The kingdom of God, like the seed in the parable, has tremendous potential for multiplication. This fact can make farming profitable. The gospel, when sown and received in human hearts, multiplies profusely.

Jesus predicted that His church, like the mustard seed, would begin small and grow into a plant big enough to encompass the whole mass of humanity. It would provide in its friendly branches a space for the poor, the outcasts of every nation.

Whatever else our Lord had in mind, it is clear He envisioned His church growing into a massive organism. Those of us who are part of the Kingdom's work must think big, act boldly, and sow broadly, for that is God's wish for His church.

Increasingly, as I go visiting nowadays, I find myself having to defend our church for being big. It is almost as if people think big is bad. Don't become suspicious of a church because it is growing. Suspect it otherwise. Growth is consistent with what Jesus expected and predicted. Our part in the process? The parable of the blades tells us it is to sow the seed and to reap the harvest. If the seed is planted in good soil where it can take root, it will grow spontaneously and inevitably. All the farmer need do is plant it. So it is with the kingdom of God. The Word of God, if given the opportunity and the right conditions, will do its own work in human hearts. Outside instrumentality is limited to two processes: first, sowing and then reaping. Between these initial and final activities, it is a matter of confidence in the vitality of the seed.

No one but God knows what a seed really is or how it changes into a flower, but we humans do know that if we will faithfully plant the seed in good soil it will grow.

Since the parable of the blades talks about going to sleep at night, rising up in the morning, and going about the normal activities of life, you might get the idea that it is an encouragement to laziness. Not so! The parable is not spoken to make the workers of the Kingdom lazy but to encourage us to more intense efforts.

If the work can't fail, if success is assured, it is a tremendous encouragement to diligence, faithfulness, and optimism in God's work.

Let those, then, who are called to sow the seed, take heart. You can go to sleep, rise up, and not be anxious about the results. They will come. No need to feel pressure to produce. There is no reason to burn yourself out. Growth in the Kingdom takes time, but it will come if we sow and faint not. The Kingdom laborers must remind themselves that the seed and the soil have the elements of life in them, and our job is to scatter faithfully and wait patiently.

Neither the farmer nor the pastor can take the responsibility or the glory for growth. Only God can cause growth. But like the farmer, the pastor is responsible for the soil. No seed can flourish in poor soil, and no church can grow unless the environment within the church is conducive to growth. As a farmer can do much to the soil—plow it, fertilize it, weed it, irrigate it—so we can do much to create a climate for growth in the church. But the power of growth God has put in His own hands. As the apostle Paul penned, "I have planted, Apollos watered; but God gave the increase" (1 Cor. 3:6). Christian workers then can look forward to the harvest if they have been faithful in sowing.

Let the worker who wants to grow an evangelistic church remember this: the gospel seed is always powerful. Our role is to work the field where God has put us. Let us cultivate it by visitation, water it with the tears of concern, create a warm and loving climate in our churches so growth can occur, and then plant the seed faithfully. If we do these, growth will come.

To grow an evangelistic church, we must do four things: preach the whole gospel to the whole world by the whole church with our whole hearts.

The Whole Gospel

The gospel is a gospel of salvation, of sanctification, and of service. Our first responsibility is to preach that whole gospel.

The gospel is first the gospel of salvation. The simplest statement of the gospel is this: "God was in Christ, reconciling the world unto himself" (2 Cor. 5:19). Our world is in rebellion against its Creator, and you and I are a part of that rebellion. By our own free will and our own personal choices, we have disobeyed God. We have broken His laws, and thus we are alienated from Him. In this condition we are hopelessly and helplessly lost. The good news is that God loves us, and while we were sinners, He acted through Christ to redeem us.

Paul declared, "When we were yet without strength, in due

time Christ died for the ungodly" (Rom. 5:6). The phrase "without strength" means that we were powerless to save ourselves. We humans can do many things on our own. We can build a rocket that will go to the moon and back. We can build a submarine that will sail around the world under water. And we can build a satellite that will beam messages instantaneously around the globe.

But there is one thing that we cannot do for ourselves. We cannot save ourselves. There is no way anybody can ever be saved apart from the grace of God. When God found us helplessly and hopelessly lost, because of His great love and mercy, He reached down to us through Jesus Christ and reconciled us to Himself. And if one will turn from one's sins and put trust in Christ, one can be saved now. That's good news!

But that is not the whole gospel. The gospel not only involves salvation—it also involves sanctification. Conversion is the end of the Christian life, but it is the front end. When we have told people how to be saved, we must then help them grow to maturity in the Christian life. The conversion of the soul is the miracle of a moment; the growth of a saint is the task of a lifetime.

After salvation and sanctification, we must move on to service. We are saved by grace through faith, and we are now God's workmanship, created unto good works.

In the early part of the twentieth century, there was a hot controversy between liberals and fundamentalists. The fundamentalists were preaching, "Get saved." The liberals were preaching, "Get involved." I believe that each side came away from the debate with only half the gospel. The fundamentalists held only to the half that saves the soul; the modernists held only to the half that ministers to the body. But we must put the pieces back together again and proclaim the whole and living gospel that declares, "Get saved, and then get involved." We can be saved through faith in the finished work of Christ, but God then expects us to become "zealous of good works."

The Whole World

We must preach the whole gospel to the whole world. Before Jesus ascended into heaven He challenged, "Ye shall be witnesses unto me both in Jerusalem, and in all Judaea, and in Samaria, and unto the uttermost part of the earth" (Acts 1:8).

He expected the gospel to be taken into the whole world, but before the church was able to "go" into all the world in obedience to this command, God brought the world to the church. Over fourteen national groups of languages were present at Pentecost (Acts 2:9-12). And churches grew up like mustard seed plants spreading their branches wherever the new converts returned after this great feast.

God is doing again in our time what He did then. We no longer have to go to the ends of the earth to witness to the ends of the earth. God is bringing the nations of the world to our doorsteps to hear the gospel in the form of immigrants, refugees, and foreign students. In fact, someone has estimated that there are in the neighborhood of one million foreign students studying here in the United States from countries other than Latin America. What a staggering missionary potential that is!

We cannot carry the gospel into most Moslem countries. But the majority of those countries that will not admit Christian missionaries send their best young people by the hundreds of thousands into our neighborhoods. Those of us who have an interest in missions overseas should ask ourselves whether God has put us at home to participate in foreign missions in our own living room and at our own meal tables.

It costs many thousands of dollars to train, equip, and support an American missionary in a foreign land. What better missionaries to send abroad than one whose target country is his or her own home? They already speak the language fluently.

They already understand the details and pitfalls of the culture. They are already immune to the diseases, and they will readily be accepted as legitimate members of their society. These returning Christian students do not have to adjust to a new climate or a new culture. They can obtain good jobs and take their places in their home communities. They can be living proof of the international quality of the gospel.

While Jesus gave the Jewish church the commission to go into all the world and make disciples of every nation, they did not do it. What Jesus spoke and what they heard were two different matters. They heard a mandate to preach the gospel to *their own kind* everywhere.

So they went to Jews only—not to other races. The Lord had to appear to Simon Peter in a special vision and send him to the house of Cornelius, a full-blooded Gentile, and show Peter that salvation was also for the Gentiles. I can imagine some of the charter members of the church sitting around commenting, "What is the church coming to?" I'll tell you what it was coming to: it was coming to a state of obedience. The gospel is for the whole world.

Similarly today, American churches are guilty of taking the gospel only to the American middle-class Anglo-Saxons. We have not usually understood the Great Commission to include all the diverse cultures so prevalent in America.

The acceptance of different ethnic backgrounds and lifestyles did not come easily to the New Testament church, and we should not expect it to be easy for us. But by 1988 there will be sixty-two million ethnics in America. We must start new churches among them or blend them into our own churches, for that's where the population growth will transpire. We simply cannot have an Archie Bunker mentality toward those who are different from us. Archie Bunker is the premier bigot-type of American. That's what makes Archie's life a series of interesting stories. He must deal with black neighbors, a Jewish shopkeeper, an atheist son-in-law, and an Oriental pastor. That's the kind of world we live in and must minister to also. Those people are a part of the world to which we must carry the gospel.

The Whole Church

We must preach the whole gospel to the whole world by the whole church. Recently, our church enlarged its existing sanctuary to double the seating capacity. Our sanctuary was rectangular in shape with a balcony across the back of it. The enlargement project consisted of moving the side walls out thirty feet on each side and horseshoeing the balcony around both sides of the sanctuary.

The construction was carried on in such a way that we were able to continue worshiping in the building throughout the entire project. The contractors first poured the outside foundation for the new sections and then erected the structural steel. Next, the steel beams for the balcony were put in place and were stuck through holes in the existing walls, and for several months they protruded out into the sanctuary.

While other work was going on, the carpenters then began to put the wooden risers for the balcony floor on the steel runners outside the existing wall. And for awhile they looked like the bleachers of a high school football stadium stuck on the sides of our sanctuary.

During this stage of construction, someone drove by our church one day and commented, "That Green Acres is the most accommodating church in the world. Look, they are building bleachers for their spectator Christians!"

Spectator Christians are one of the major problems every church faces. Too many Christians are content to sit in the grandstands of life and give an occasional cheer or boo, but they never become involved. It is high time we climbed out of the grandstands and onto the playing field of life.

If we are going to win the world to Christ, we must reclaim

the principle of every Christian's being a witness. I know that thought must scare some of you to death. As Paul Little says in his book *How To Give Away Your Faith,* all of us have made awkward attempts at witnessing, and we have come away feeling as unnerved as an elephant on ice; because of our traumatic experiences, we withdraw and cop out on the ministry of witnessing. Most of us Christians don't know how to move out into our world. Instead, we have withdrawn from it. So, while 98 percent of us sit back and let the "pros" or the "gifted" do the job, the gospel continues to be little known and still less believed.

This will not make it. We must have the whole gospel preached to the whole world by the whole church.

The Whole Heart

Finally, we must do this with our whole hearts. American churches tend toward two extremes: sterile intellectualism and empty emotionalism. There is a need for our churches to have a faith that is a healthy blend of the mind, the heart, and the spirit.

The element of zeal must be recaptured in our churches if we are to be effective for Christ. Paul declared that the Lord gave Himself to redeem us from sin and to purify unto Himself a people who would be "zealous" of good works (Titus 2:14).

There is no reason for the world to have a monopoly on enthusiasm. But it must not be unbridled and wild-eyed. Enthusiasm can be appealing or appalling, depending on how it is expressed. The Scriptures warn us that if the church doesn't wake up and warm up, our Lord is going to throw up! (Rev. 3:16). Our task then is clear. We are to preach the whole gospel to the whole world by the whole church with our whole hearts. That is what we are to be about. So let's have a go at it. Instead of writing more books about what is wrong with the church, let's become the church.

Instead of trying to impress people with how much better we are than some others we know, let's try being human. Let's concentrate our efforts on bringing our non-Christian friends into some kind of atmosphere where they can learn how Christ will put their lives back together.

Let's start holding guests' nights, bringing in visiting evangelists for preaching missions, or working with other churches in citywide crusades.

Let's have a go at honesty. Instead of trying to appear to be holy, dignified, and sophisticated, let's melt some of the "stuffed-shirtedness" out of the church and tell the world that whatever good is being done by Christianity is God's doing, not ours. Let's take another look at the New Testament to see what "separation" actually means and how Jesus walked and worked with people.

In short, let's roll up our sleeves and go to work sowing and reaping, knowing that if we sow and faint not, in due season we shall reap. That's how to grow an evangelistic church.

5
Knowing the Times
and Meeting the Needs

You and I happen to share this planet, and we have been called to minister for Christ in the most explosive time in history. Powerful tides are surging across much of our world today, creating a new, often bizarre, environment in which to work, play, marry, raise children, or retire. Value systems are splintering and crashing while the lifeboats of family, church, and faith are hurled madly about.

If we are going to grow evangelistic churches today, then we must understand the times, so we will understand what we ought to do. This has always been a prerequisite for effective service.

The Bible gives us an example of this in 1 Chronicles 12:32. It says of the men of Issachar that they had an "understanding of the times, to know what Israel ought to do." This statement is from the list of brave men of Israel who attached themselves to David at Hebron and made him king during the waning days of King Saul's reign. The men of Issachar are given special mention because of their spiritual insight and practical statesmanship. They made the right estimation of their times and helped elevate David to the throne. Because they understood their times, they knew what action needed to be taken by the people of God.

We must have the same understanding today. America began as an agricultural society. The agricultural society had its be-

ginning about 8000 BC and continued into the 1700s: an era of
almost ten thousand years.

Then in the early 1700s the industrial society was born. Great
factories sprang up, and people started moving from rural areas
into the city—from farming to manufacturing. The industrial
era continued until the 1950s.

But today, only nine percent of the laboring force in America
is engaged in the manufacturing of goods. We have now moved
into what is called "the information society." Almost everyone
who is added to today's labor force is involved somehow in the
collection, assimilation, and distribution of information. Our
age is characterized by satellites, cable television, and computers.

According to Dr. Carl Hammer, director of computer
sciences for the Univac Division of Sperry Rand Corporation,
computers already do 99 percent of the clerical work in America. This has produced such an information glut that there are
not enough people in the entire world to handle the work of the
computers already operating in the United States.

We live in a time of instant global communication. An event
can happen in one place in the world, and in a matter of only
a few minutes, it can be known and even seen in every other
place in the world. When President Lincoln was shot, the word
was communicated by telegraph to most parts of the United
States, but because we had no link with England, it was five
days before London heard about the event. When President
Reagan was shot, journalist Henry Fairly, working at his type-
writer within a block of the shooting, received word of it by
telephone from his editor at *The Spectator* in London who had
seen a rerun of the assassination attempt on television shortly
after it had occurred.

We live in a time of tremendous speed and travel. In 1927,
when Charles Lindberg made the first solo flight across the
Atlantic, he traveled at the speed of one-hundred miles per

hour. He made the flight from New York City to Paris in thirty-three hours and twenty minutes. Not long ago, a US reconnaissance jet made essentially the same flight in one hour and forty-six minutes: traveling at an average speed of eighteen-hundred miles per hour. That's faster than a 30.06 shell is traveling when it leaves the barrel of a rifle.

This is a time of shift from national to world interest. The world economy, for example, is becoming more important than the national economy. We wear clothes made in Hong Kong; we watch televisions made in Japan; we construct buildings out of steel manufactured in Korea; we drive cars made in Germany; and we tell time by watches made in Switzerland. We are being forced more and more to think globally instead of locally.

Ours is a do-it-yourself society. We have self-service gas stations, do-it-yourself pregnancy tests, electronic banking, and check-it-yourself blood-pressure machines.

And all of these social, political, and economic changes are mirrored in personal disintegration. Marriage and the families are fighting for their lives. Half the marriages in America now end in divorce. For years the traditional family in America was thought of as a working husband, a housekeeping wife, and two children. But only seven percent of American families fit into that category today. Many people are choosing to live solo. There are more and more one-parent families, and many couples are simply choosing to live together without marriage at all.

This is a time of theological confusion. A few years ago, local pastors largely determined the theology of their people and their communities. But today many people have heard two or three preachers on television before they ever arrive at their own church for worship.

Psychotherapists and gurus are doing a land-office business as people wander aimlessly from cults to fads, convinced that reality is absurd, insane, and meaningless.

Our churches are beginning to feel the effects of all of this. In the last twenty years, six of the mainline Protestant denominations have lost a combined membership of over four million people.

Yet studies have shown that half of the nation's unchurched view themselves as potentially responsive to the church if they could find one with good preaching, a religious education program for their children, and one that was seriously concerned about working for the betterment of society.

What should we do to reach all of these people for Christ, as well as keep those we already have? What have we to offer this kind of world? What can we do to stem the decline that is all around us? In the light of our time: What should the people of God be doing? Here are four personal suggestions: hold up hope; create community; multiply our ministry; and yield to the Holy Spirit.

Hold Up Hope

First, we must emphasize hope. We are living in a time of severe anxiety. Gloom and doom are heard on every hand. Newspapers, television, and politicians all present a despairing picture of today's world.

Our role as the church is not to echo the despair and anxiety in secular society around us but to hold up hope. We must tell people about the grace of God that offers to them the possibility of a new life. Their sins can be forgiven; they can have victory over habits and circumstances; they can have divine guidance in the making of their decisions; and they can have the assurance of heaven when they die. That is the hope people need and seek.

The New Testament is a book of hope based on resurrection theology. This is not "Pollyannaish." It is based on the conviction that our ultimate destiny is in the hands of God. The same power that raised Jesus from the dead is alive and available in our world today.

But many of our churches mirror the despair of the age rather than proclaim the hope. I was driving down the highway the other day and saw a sign with an arrow pointed down a country road that said, "Little Hope Baptist Church—3 miles." I thought to myself, *My soul, I'm glad I'm not the pastor of that church.* If I were, my first action would be to start a movement to change its name. I would have them call it: "Big Hope Baptist Church" or "New Hope Baptist Church," or "Living Hope Baptist Church," or "Coming Hope Baptist Church" or "Everlasting Hope Baptist Church," or "Glorious Hope Baptist Church," or "Flaming Hope Baptist Church"—anything but "Little Hope Baptist Church."

The only name worse than "Little Hope Baptist Church" would be "No Hope Baptist Church." That's exactly what many of our churches are presenting to the world today: little or no hope.

People need faith, courage, and assurance for the difficult task of living in today's world. And they will gravitate to the place where that is found. If we will hold up hope, our despairing world can be reached.

Create Community

The second thing we need to do is create community. There are three basic needs that every person has. Everyone needs meaning, structure, and community. People are not content just to exist; we must have purpose, a cause beyond ourselves and greater than ourselves to live for.

People also need structure, discipline, and guidelines for their lives. But most of all, they need community. We need a sense of belonging, of being a part of a group where we are known, accepted, and loved.

In our society, loneliness looms like an iceberg, chilling the waters of life all around us. Never before in history have people lived so close together and yet felt so far apart. We travel down crowded highways, rush through packed airports, shop in crowded malls, live in crowded apartment complexes, and still we are lonely. People everywhere yearn for a personal touch, a sense of belonging.

Loneliness is not the absence of people; it is the absence of meaningful personal relationships. It is the feeling that you are unknown, unloved, and unimportant.

Jean Nidetch, who founded Weight Watchers of America, gave insight into her one-time obesity when she stated,

> I always feel as if I am just on the fringe of understanding why I got fat. People are hungry for one another; maybe that's why I ate. I wanted to fill the void. I keep telling my daughter-in-law, "Hug that little baby of yours, kiss her, hold her close, don't let her be hungry for love."
>
> We are all looking for something, maybe religion, maybe a guy. I don't know. But it sure isn't a hunk of chocolate cake. (from *Reader's Digest*, "Personal Glimpses," Barbara Grizzuti Harrison in *McCall's*.)

Who can better provide a caring and sharing fellowship, a community where people are loved and accepted than the local church? Bars can't. Clubs and fraternities can't. And the electronic church can't. The electronic church may provide better music and better preaching than the local church can, but it cannot offer the one thing that the human spirit most hungers for—the human touch.

This need for community is the secret to the success of the cults. It is loosely estimated today that some three million Americans belong to more than one thousand religious cults. Why do many thousands of apparently intelligent, seemingly successful people allow themselves to be sucked into the myriad of cults sprouting today? What accounts for the total control that a Jim Jones was able to exercise over the lives of his followers? Why is it that such groups can command almost total dedication and obedience from their members? The secret is simple. They understand the need for community, structure, and meaning. For these are what all the cults peddle.

The cults offer meaning to people's lives. Each has its own single-minded version of reality: religious, political, or cultural. The cult believes that it possesses the sole truth. The "meaning" delivered by the cult may be absurd to the outsider, but that doesn't matter. It provides meaning to the person on the inside.

The cult offers much-needed structure. Cults impose tight constraints on behavior. They demand and create an enormous discipline of their followers. Our society is so permissive, and people have so many options to chose from that they cannot make their own decisions effectively. They want others to make their decisions for them, and thus they will follow them.

Most of all, the cults offer lonely people community. In the beginning, the newcomer is surrounded by people offering friendship and beaming approval. So powerful and rewarding is this sudden warmth and attention that cult members are often willing to give up everything and everyone for it.

But no one has the potential for community like the church. We have been called together by the Spirit of God, to do the will of God, and to be the family of God. If we offer the world genuine Christian love, we can reach people today.

We live in a cold world, but people are still drawn by the warmth of love and fellowship. It is the responsibility of all of us to reach out to those in our neighborhoods, apartment complexes, and especially those who walk through the doors of our churches and make them feel welcome in the family.

Multiply Ministry

The church is not only the family of God, it is also the body of Jesus Christ on earth today. We are to busy ourselves, then, in doing what He did in the days of His flesh. What did Jesus do? The Scriptures indicate that He went about doing good (Acts 10:38). We must therefore not be content merely to go about. We must reach out to alcoholics, to distraught parents, to the unemployed, to the brokenhearted, to the oppressed, to the imprisoned, and do all we can in the name of Christ to help them.

Doing the gospel is not only our most powerful witness, but it is also the hope of bringing back a sense of community which twentieth-century theology has all but stripped away from us. We Christians must exercise the power of forming personal relationships with social outcasts from every walk of life. The basis of our ministry begins with God's love for humanity.

We must go to them because they are men and women who need to know Christ's love for them. And the only way they will ever experience that love is for us to demonstrate it by going to them as God commanded us to do. We are God's people, and we care because He cares. The object of life is not the pursuit of gain or the fulfillment of self, but the service of Christ.

When John the Baptist was imprisoned by Herod, he began to have doubts about Jesus' Messiahship. John, you remember, was the first bold witness for Christ. He had declared, "Behold the Lamb of God, who takes away the sin of the world!" (John 1:29, RSV). But then, sometime later, John had doubts. So he sent two of his disciples to ask, "Art thou he that should come, or do we look for another?" (Matt. 11:3).

Jesus' response was,

> Go and shew John again those things which ye do hear and see: The blind receive their sight, and the lame walk, the lepers are cleansed, and the deaf hear, the dead are raised up, and the poor have the gospel preached to them (vv. 4-5).

The essence of Jesus' answer to John was this: Tell John about My ministry, and when he knows what I am doing, he will know who I am. As it was with Jesus, so it should be with us. Our ministry should mark us as the Master's people.

The Lord Jesus met people as they were, not as they ought to have been. Angry young men, blind beggars, proud politicians, loose-living streetwalkers, dirty and naked victims of demonism, and grieving parents all received equal time. The hungry, the sick, the outcasts, the despairing all came to realize the grace of God in Christ, came to know God in Christ's cross, and came to believe God in Christ's resurrection from the dead.

As Christ was among persons ministering, so we must be among them. George MacCleod put it this way:

> I simply argue that the cross be raised again
> At the center of the marketplace
> As well as on the steeple of the church,
>
> I am recovering the claim that
> Jesus was not crucified in a cathedral
> Between two candles:
> But on a cross between two thieves;
> On a town garbage heap;
> At a crossroads of politics so cosmopolitan
> That they had to write his title in
> Hebrew and Latin and Greek . . .
>
> At the kind of place where cynics talk smut
> And thieves curse and soldiers gamble.
> Because that is where He died,
> And that is what he died about,
> That is where Christ's men ought to be,
> And what Christ's people ought to be about.

Everywhere people are hurting; everywhere marriages are falling apart; everywhere people are in the grips of alcohol and drugs; everywhere young people are discouraged with life; everywhere parents are distraught. In such a world we must be busy ministering as Jesus did. That is the only way to win our world to Christ.

Yield to the Holy Spirit

Finally, we must emphasize the Holy Spirit. The Holy Spirit is the Spirit of power, of love, of truth, and of life. Wherever the Spirit of God moves and works, there will be life and power.

Years ago John Henry Giles wanted to preach a sermon on "The Wind Blows Where It Will." So he went down to the docks of his city and asked an old sailor friend, a seasoned salt with a weather-beaten face, to tell him about the wind.

He wanted to discover where the wind came from, how the wind worked, and how to control the wind.

His old seaman friend mused, "Oh, preacher, I don't know the answer to those questions. I don't know where the wind comes from. I don't know how the wind works. And I sure don't know how to control the wind."

"You mean to tell me," responded the preacher, "that you have sailed the seven seas, you have spent your life living by the winds, and you don't know those things?"

"No, preacher," answered the old sailor, "I don't know how the wind works, but I do know one thing. I know how to hoist my sail to catch the wind. And when I do, it takes me wherever I need to go."

The movement of the Holy Spirit in the world is like the unpredictable, uncontrollable wind moving across the surface of time. Our task is not to control the Holy Spirit's work but to ride the winds of His power when we encounter them.

We don't know a lot about the Holy Spirit. We don't understand how He works, and we surely don't have control over Him. It is true: "The wind bloweth where it listeth" (John 3:8).

But we can work in harmony with Him, allowing Him to control, to direct, and to empower our lives and our churches.

Only as we do this can we win our world to Christ. In our

day, as in the days of David, we need people like the men of Issachar who have an understanding of the times, to know what the people of God ought to do. The more I discern the times, the more I sense the need to hold up hope, create community, multiply ministry, and to yield to the Holy Spirit. That's how to grow an evangelistic church.

6
Worship that Wins

In the sixteenth century the Church of England was steeped in ritualistic worship. Then along came John and Charles Wesley who taught the people to sing robust songs unto the Lord and preached soul-stirring sermons that broke England out of the meaningless ritual of their day. The people turned back to God, and England was saved from the age of reason that eventually devastated France.

Wesley once reported in his diary:

Preached this morning at 6:00 a.m. to 1200 ministers and was thrown out of the church.

Preached at 10:00 A.M. to a crowd and it was totally unsuccessful.

Preached at 2:00 P.M. and they hated me.

Preached at 5:00 P.M. and the response was negative.

Preached at 10:00 P.M. and had one-hundred fifty saved.

Praise God, the ritualistic church was not there to get in my way.

Ritualistic worship almost always stands in the way of reaching people for Christ. So to grow an evangelistic church we must pay attention to worship. It is one of the most important keys to reaching and keeping people.

The importance of worship was emphasized by Jesus when He declared, "True worshippers shall worship the Father in

spirit and in truth: for the Father seeketh such to worship him"
(John 4:23).

The two words *spirit* and *truth* give emphasis to how we
worship rather than where we worship. To worship in *spirit* is
to worship with our inner being. Worship is an attitude, not
only an act, an emotion, not only a motion. Worship is much
deeper than merely being physically present in church, hearing
a sermon, listening to music, or mingling with people. We can
do all of those and still not make an inward response to God.
It is possible to be absent (in mind) at the precise time we take
up the most space. For worship to be real, our spirits must
respond to God's Spirit. To worship in truth is to worship in
consistency with God's nature.

We should always let the nature of God determine the nature
of our worship. That means we should eliminate from our
services those elements inconsistent with His nature and incor-
porate in our worship those that are.

What is God like? We need to know in order to develop
meaningful worship experiences. I do not see God as cold,
remote, austere, dull, or impersonal. Do you? Worship, then,
that reflects God should be warm, personal, alive, joyous, and
enthusiastic, just as God is.

Such worship is basic to growing an evangelistic church that
wins and keeps converts. Growth, at its best, is a by-product of
this kind of worship. That's how it was in Acts. That's how it
ought to be today.

So if you want to grow an evangelistic church, let your
worship be deeply spiritual and consistent with the nature of
God.

Music with "Guts"

The kind of worship that will win and hold people is alive,
dynamic, and enthusiastic. After all, we serve a living God.

How then can our worship be dead and listless and at the same time convey the truth about Him?

Real worship ought to be the celebration of life. Early Christian worship was informal, spontaneous, joyous, and even exuberant on occasions. It was only much later after the church began to backslide that worship stiffened into a great formality and was clouded by a sense of gloom.

The worship of early Christians was filled with the joy of a new life in Christ Jesus, and that helped them grow both numerically and spiritually. It will help us today.

Some ministers conduct public worship as if the only people present were mourners or victims of some recent or impending tragedy. To do this is to forget the very nature of God. If God is the Giver of life, the Sustainer of life, and the Redeemer of life, then the worship of Him should be a celebration of life, and it should be with joy. People should not only bring their sorrows to church but also their shouts of joy and victory.

One of the best places to begin to add life and joy to your worship is with music.

Not long ago I called on a family who had recently visited our church. For years they had been a part of a ritualistic church. The man of the house had recently become a Christian, and he was no longer satisfied with his former church.

He said to me, "I really like your church, especially the music. You sing music with guts."

I had never heard anyone say anything like that before in my life. I had heard of people with guts, and I had heard of gasoline with guts. But I had never heard of music with guts.

However, I understood exactly what he meant. He meant that our music has a message to it. It has heart and soul, and we sing it with gusto.

To me, there are no great churches without great music, and there is no great music without great enthusiasm.

How can the choir sing gloomy, mournful anthems, the congregation sing in a listless, halfhearted way, and the church convey the truth about God to a lost world? The growing churches are those that sing triumphant and victorious hymns joyously and enthusiastically.

Check Your Flyleaf

Just as there are no great churches without great singing, so there are no great churches without great fellowship. Since our God is warm and loving, our churches ought to be warm and loving. People who are cold and aloof are not true representatives of our Heavenly Father. If a church lacks warmth and friendliness it will never reach and keep people. Robert Burns, the poet, visited a church one Sunday and wrote his feelings in the flyleaf of a hymnal:

> As cold a wind as ever blew;
> A colder church, and in it but few;
> As cold a minister as ever spak':
> Ye'll all be hot ere I come back.

Some churches need to check their flyleafs to see what visitors are writing there. Vacant pews may tell us something about our fellowship or lack of it.

I have read in a number of church bulletins the invitation: "To all that mourn and need comfort; to all who are weary and need rest; to all who are friendless and want friendship; to all who are homesick and want sheltering love—this church opens wide the door and makes a place, saying, 'Welcome in the name of Jesus Christ our Lord.' "

When that is the true spirit of people, not just words, we can grow an evangelistic church.

If you were to visit our church and see our people laughing and talking with one another before the worship services begin, you might feel that we were irreverent. Some people think we ought to enter the sanctuary and sit quietly with our heads bowed until the services begin.

Personally, I have never seen any logic in asking two thousand-plus people together to sit and be quiet. If you want to sit and be quiet, do that at home by yourself. The church is the family of God. The worship service should be much like a family reunion. When we come together as a church, we ought to visit with one another and enjoy one another. When it's time for the service to begin, people have no problem quieting down to hear what God has to share through His Word.

Greet the Visitors

We add to the warmth and friendliness of our church by having a visitors' reception after each of our worship services. At the close of the invitation and before we introduce our new members, I say something like this to the congregation: "We welcome again those of you who visit with us today. We always end our worship with a reception for visitors in my study. I hope you can stay for a few minutes after this service so I can shake your hand and have a cup of coffee with you." Then I give them directions to my study and say, "Some of our deacons and their wives will be there to meet you and serve you. I will be there as soon as I greet the people at the front door. I'll look forward to seeing you there."

Usually ten to twenty visitors will stay for these receptions each week. Two of our deacons and their wives are in charge of each of the receptions. They prepare the coffee, serve the guests, place name tags on them, and then introduce me to them when I arrive.

I have the reception in my study because it adds another personal touch to our church. The people identify with me and with the church better than if we were in a parlor or the library.

In these receptions, I make many valuable contacts for our church and even lead people to Christ occasionally.

We also have a new members' fellowship in my home once a month. We have this following an evening worship service for all those who have joined our church during the previous month. This, too, is led by our deacons. They send out the invitations, greet the people at the door, and prepare and serve the refreshments.

After all have been served, we then circle the room asking guests to introduce themselves and to share something about their lives. I then welcome them as a part of our Green Acres family and challenge them to be faithful to Christ and His church.

In a large church such as ours, many people never know where the pastor lives, much less ever visit in his home. That's why I insist on having this fellowship in my home. Having it there adds another personal touch to our ministry.

Don't Talk Junk

Not long ago a little girl in our church wrote me a note. She commented, "I like you very much because you don't talk junk." I'm not sure all she meant by that, but it really sounded good.

We live in a world where people eat junk food, read junk books, watch junk movies, listen to junk music, and we wonder why they become junkies. The churches that reach and keep people don't have junk preaching. They are churches that preach and teach the Word of God in a clear and authoritative manner.

Since God is truth, our worship must center in truth. That means that the preaching and teaching of God's Word must be at the very heart of real worship.

Preaching at its best is relevant and down to earth. It moves out of the realm of the theoretical and into the realm of the practical. The concern of most people is not how to worship in the catacombs but how to remain human in the skyscrapers.

They aren't interested in pie in the sky by-and-by. They are concerned about a chicken in the kitchen today.

Our preaching should be plain and simple. We are feeding sheep, not giraffes, so put the message down where they can reach it. Don't try to be some kind of arch-intellectual. As one man expressed it: "Aim low; they are riding Shetlands."

We should preach with a sense of urgency. Each time we go into the pulpit, it should be as though it were the first time . . . as though it were the best time . . . and for sure as though it could be the last time.

We should make it interesting. George Jessel's advice for public speakers applies to us: "If you haven't struck oil in the first three minutes, stop boring."

Above all, it should always include an appeal for people to respond to Christ's call to salvation and discipleship. Somewhere I read, "When you preach, never leave Christ on the cross or the prodigal son in the far country." That's good—really good. Never close without giving people hope and inviting them to new life in Christ.

To rivet the truth of the sermon in the minds of our people, I encourage them to take notes on my sermons. Our bulletin is a threefold page with the last page left blank for taking sermon notes. Since people can listen three to ten times as fast as you can speak, they have a lot of time on their hands during the worship service. Taking notes on the sermons helps them to concentrate as well as retain what is being said.

After I have given the introduction to my sermon, and I am ready to present the body of the message I say something like this, "If you are taking notes on the sermon, as I encourage you to do, these are the things you will want to write down . . ." Then I give them the main points of my message. The title and the text have already been printed in the bulletin. Hopefully they will have written these down earlier. Now with an outline

in mind, they can follow along and fill in anything else they may
want to keep.

Enter to Worship, Depart to Serve

I was in Belize, Central America, a few months ago on a
mission trip. I preached one night at the Calvary Baptist
Church of Belize City. As I entered the church I noticed a sign
above the door that read: "Enter to worship." Once inside I
noticed a sign on the opposite side of the door that read: "De-
part to serve."

Worship and work are opposite sides of the same coin. They
are not competitors but companions. They don't conflict—they
complement. Effective service requires worship. Effective worship inspires service.

Worship that ends only in hymn singing, handshaking, and
sermon listening falls far short of the divine ideal. Our God is
One Who acts. Therefore worship that does not issue forth into
action is an incomplete and inadequate worship.

A cowboy explained his idea of Christian worship and service
like this: "Now, I'm working for Jim here. If I'd sit around
telling what a good fellow Jim is and singing songs for Jim, I
would be doing just what a lot of Christians do; but I wouldn't
suit Jim, and I would get fired mighty quick. But when I buckle
on my chaps and hustle among the hills and see that Jim's herd
is all right and not suffering from lack of water or feed or getting
off the range and branded by cattle thieves, then I'm proving
my loyalty and serving Jim as he wants to be served."

Isaiah ended his worship experience saying, "Here am I;
[Lord,] send me" (6:8). That kind of decisiveness should mark
every true worship experience.

Genuine worship, the kind that reflects the nature of God,
always issues forth into practical service and loving ministry to
others.

How do we grow an evangelistic church? A large part of the

secret is to have worship that is warm and personal, joyful and enthusiastic, spiritual and practical, and that centers in the truth of God's Word.

That's what built the church in the Book of Acts, and that's what will build it today.

7
Go-Givers
in a Go-Getter World

It was spoken of Knute Rockne, the legendary football coach, "In an age that has stamped itself as an era of the 'go-getter,' Knute Rockne was a 'go-giver.' "

Go-givers in a go-getter world—that's what it takes to grow an evangelistic church. Those who lead, as well as those who follow, must move out of the realm of the superficial and into the realm of the sacrificial. We must become servants of God and of humanity.

While I have already talked much about leadership in this book, the more I have studied the subject the more I realize that leadership as such is never exalted in the Word of God. Instead, service is honored and revered.

In the King James Version of the Bible, for example, the term *leader* occurs only six times. That is not to say that the theme is not prominent in the Bible, but it is usually referred to in different terms, the most prominent being "servant." It is not "Moses, My leader" but "Moses, My servant." This emphasis is consonant with the teaching of Christ that we are to lead by serving.

John spoke of the servanthood of Christ when he wrote,

> So after he had washed their feet, and had taken his garments, and was set down again, he said unto them, Know ye not what I have done to you? Ye call me Master and Lord: and ye say

well; for so I am. If I then, your Lord and Master, have washed
your feet; ye also ought to wash one another's feet. For I have
given you an example, that ye should do as I have done to you.
Verily, verily, I say unto you, The servant is not greater than
his lord; neither he that is sent greater than he that sent him.
If ye know these things, happy are ye if you do them (John
13:12-17).

The scene is the upper room. The occasion is the Passover
and the Last Supper. The supper is over, and the disciples are
talking among themselves, seemingly unaware of the events
that are about to occur. Jesus, however, is keenly aware, realiz-
ing He will soon be taken out of the world. As He thinks on
this, He also reflects on how much He loves His disciples. And
with this thought in mind, while they are still chatting with one
another, Jesus arises from the supper table, girds Himself with
a towel, pours a bowl of water, and begins to wash His disciples'
feet. In so doing He is assuming the role of a servant.

In Jesus' day the only shoes people had were sandals. Since
there were no cement sidewalks and no asphalt streets, as persons walked from place to place their feet would get dirty. So
when people arrived at their destinations, they were met at the
door by a slave who washed the dust or the mud from their feet.
Foot washing was a servant's work. Jesus was assuming the role
of a servant as He washed His disciples' feet.

When He finished, He put the bowl and towel aside and sat
down again. Then He asked His disciples, "Do you know what
I have done to you?" (v. 12, RSV). The question was asked to
arrest their attention; to rivet their mind on what He was about
to say to them. Then He said, "Ye call me Master and Lord:
and ye say well; for so I am" (v. 13). Jesus was fully conscious
of Who He was. But that was not enough. The disciples also
needed to be reminded of who He was.

They needed this consciousness for two reasons: first, it was
only as they understood Who He was that they could under-

stand the significance of what He had done. The Lord of glory, their Master, had assumed the role of a slave and had stooped to wash their feet. Knowing who He was gave greater significance to what He had done.

But they also needed to be reminded that He was Lord and Master to underscore His authority. He was about to teach them a revolutionary new truth. Reminding them that He was Lord and Master would help them to accept the truth more readily.

Then Jesus said, "If I then, your Lord and Master, have washed your feet; ye also ought to wash one another's feet" (v. 14).

I want you to note the word *ought.* It is used fifteen times in the New Testament and means "to be obligated" or "to be indebted to." Paul used it in reference to marriage when he wrote that husbands ought to love their wives as they love their own bodies. The writer of Hebrews used it in reference to maturity and reproved his readers for still needing to be taught when they ought to be teachers themselves.

The apostle John used it in reference to missions when he wrote that we ought to support missionaries, for by so doing we become allies with them in the gospel. And Jesus used the same word in reference to ministry.

So we have in the Bible the *ought* of marriage, the *ought* of maturity, the *ought* of missions, and the *ought* of ministry.

Then Jesus added, "For I have given you an example, that ye should do as I have done" (v. 15). Mark also used the word *example.* Jesus, in using it, claimed not only to be our Lord and Master but also our example. He is not only the God we worship and the king we obey, He is also the example we copy. We are to do what He did: we are to pattern our lives and ministries after Him.

Jesus concluded His teaching with this beautitude: "If ye know these things, happy are ye if ye do them" (v. 17).

In washing His disciples' feet, Jesus was not giving us another ordinance like baptism or the Lord's Supper. We understand this because of the absence of references to foot washing in the Epistles. Only once, in 1 Timothy 5:10, is foot washing mentioned in Scripture after this. So, obviously, it was not a common practice among New Testament Christians. But the Lord's Supper and baptism are referred to often.

It is the spirit, not the mere act of Christ, that He wants us to copy. It is His life and ministry of servanthood that must be a pattern for us.

This practice of servanthood may be the most neglected teaching of Jesus in the contemporary church. Among Christian leaders today we have too many big-time operators and too few servants. If we are going to grow evangelistic churches, we must take Jesus as our role model and become servants ourselves.

We can't sit around in plush offices and act like religious big shots, waiting for people to come to us. We've got to climb down out of our ivory towers, from behind our stained-glass windows, and mix in the sin and din of the world.

We can't act like petty tyrants or tinhorn dictators expecting people to serve us, honor us, and applaud us. We must do again in our day what Jesus did in His day: stoop and serve.

We must love people, visit people, care for people, spend, and be spent for them. We must forget about ourselves, our reputations, our ease, and think about others. We must pattern our lives after the Lord of glory, the Master of all, who stooped to take the role of a servant and washed His disciples' feet.

What are the marks of this kind of ministry? What characterizes the servant Christ, and what ought to characterize His servants today? There are three marks that identify the servant spirit of Jesus that we need: a loving heart, an humble mind, and a sacrificial spirit.

If You Want Joy, Real Joy

Everything Jesus did in His life and ministry was rooted in love. John told us at the outset of this experience that Jesus "having loved his own which were in the world, he loved them unto the end" (v. 1).

Out of love for His disciples He stooped to wash their feet. Love is the fountain from which all Jesus did flowed. Love must also be the fountain from which your ministry flows; otherwise, it will not be characterized by either joy or effectiveness.

Love is not only eternal; it is also day to day. It not only brings home the bacon; it fries it! Then it washes the skillet afterwards. When you love people in this practical, down-to-earth way, they will listen to you and follow you.

The test of your effectiveness as a Christian leader and minister will be in direct proportion to your love. People don't care how much you know until they know how much you care. Those to whom you minister may not always perfectly understand what you say, but they will soon know whether or not you love them. The secret of many successful Christian workers is not that they are skilled, knowledgeable, and have endowments which are superior to others but that those to whom they minister know that they really care about them, not in an abstract way, or from a sense of duty, but wanting with all their hearts the best that God has for them.

If we do not really love people, we will chafe under their demands. We will resent their intrusions on our time. We will whine and complain about how little they pay us and how much they expect of us. But if we really love them and serve them expecting nothing in return, we will find joy unspeakable in His service.

Have you ever seen a time when there seemed to be so little joy and so much dissatisfaction in our churches? It is because we do not love as we ought. And when we don't love as we ought, we don't serve as we ought. For it is in serving that we find our greatest joy.

Jesus ended His teaching by saying, "If ye know these things, happy are ye if ye do them" (v. 17). The deepest joy to be found in this world is in being a servant of Jesus Christ and a servant of others. If we will serve as Christ did, we will never be disappointed.

How Is Your Reputation?

The second mark of a servant is an humble mind. The apostle Paul spoke of the humble mind of Christ:

> Let this mind be in you, which was also in Christ Jesus: Who, being in the form of God, thought it not robbery to be equal with God: but made himself of no reputation, and took upon him the form of a servant, and was made in the likeness of men: And being found in fashion as a man, he humbled himself, and became obedient unto death, even the death of the cross. Wherefore God also hath highly exalted him, and given him a name which is above every name: That at the name of Jesus every knee should bow, of things in heaven, and things in earth, and things under the earth; And that every tongue should confess that Jesus Christ is Lord, to the glory of God the Father (Phil. 2:5-11).

When Paul talked about our having the mind of Christ, he was not referring to His intellectual grasp. He meant His attitude or disposition. We can never have the understanding of Jesus. We can never know all He knew, but we can have His humble spirit.

The context of this truth indicates that some of the Philippian Christians had a self-centered, righteous rigidity and pettiness that was incriminating. Insistence upon your own rights, requiring your own space, demanding that your way is best, always throwing in your two-bit's worth, claiming your own pew, and building your own kingdom may be acceptable in the world, but it is repulsive in the church.

Worldly ambition always expresses itself in three ways: building a reputation, collecting wealth, and wielding power. Its fatal flaw: it centers on self, not God.

The results of this ambition in Philippi were jealousy, envy, and factions among the believers. It always is. Most problems in churches are not caused by big men wanting to serve but by little men wanting to rule.

In stark contrast to this self-centeredness, Paul lifted up Christ who made "himself of no reputation" as an example for them to follow. Christ gave up all the rights and privileges of God and in humility stepped down to earth as a man. And He not only became a man, He humbled Himself so completely that He became identified with the criminal element of society by dying on the cross. Christ Jesus was not concerned about making a name for Himself. He left that to God. His concern was serving us. That, emphasized Paul, is the attitude, the disposition, we should all have.

It is tragic that so many who follow the Christ who forgot about His own reputation are most concerned about building theirs. They seek appointments to high places. They long to be singled out for laudatory honors; they politic for positions of authority; and they love to be called "Doctor."

This is one of the saddest aspects of modern Christianity. It is bad enough when the church is unable to change the world; it is worse when the church becomes worldly.

To His disciples who were jockeying for positions in His kingdom, Jesus explained, "Whosoever of you will be the chiefest, shall be servant of all" (Mark 10:44). Religious pyramid climbers today need to listen to those words carefully. Jesus preached that humble service is both the way to happiness and to true greatness. And it is the best way to grow an evangelistic church.

No Sacrifice—No Feast

I ran into a phrase sometime ago that stabbed me: "There was never a feast without a sacrifice." This was true for Christ who "came not to be ministered unto, but to minister, and to give His life a ransom for many" (Matt. 20:28). It is also true for us. In Christ's service we cannot succeed unless we bleed.

We cannot copy the suffering of Christ, but we can copy His service. We can die to self and live for others. Dying to self is not some mystical experience that is hard to understand. It is a practical experience that is hard to practice. It is living a selfless life rather than a selfish one. It is putting God's will and the well-being of others above ourselves.

In Jesus' service He did what He did not have to do and what no one expected Him to do, and He did it to the most unlikely of people. That's always the spirit of a true servant. Jesus washed the feet of Judas who would betray Him, of Peter who would deny Him, of Thomas who would doubt Him, and of all the rest of the apostles who would desert Him. Though He knew they would fail in their duty, He would not fail in His.

Someone has commented that the mark of big people is how they treat little people. When we have a servant's heart, no place is too small, no position is too humble, no price is too high, and no person is too insignificant for us to help.

True servants do not worry about overtime or underpay. They do not think in terms of how little they can do for Christ or for others: but how much. True servants will go the second mile, and even the third if necessary. And they will do it without bitterness or complaint.

This kind of sacrifice always marks the true servant. John Wesley, the founder of Methodism, had a motto that went like this:

> Do all the good you can,
> By all the means you can,

> In all the places you can,
> At all the times you can,
> To all the people you can,
> As long as ever you can.

Wesley's life exemplified this spirit. He was ordained at the age of twenty-four and continued to be active in the ministry for the next sixty-four years.

He preached a total of 42,400 sermons, an average of fifteen a week for fifty-four years. The average minister today preaches only about 100 sermons a year. At that rate it would take 2424 years to preach as many times as Wesley did.

Wesley traveled 290,000 miles in his lifetime. That is equal to encircling the globe over twenty times. That may not seem like many miles to the modern traveler who rides in an automobile or a jet airplane, but remember that Wesley either walked or rode on horseback most of that distance.

His writings were prolific. In all, Wesley's works, including abridgements and translations, amounted to over two-hundred volumes.

In order to accomplish all of this, Wesley daily died to himself—his own comfort, ease, and will—and lived only for Christ and others. When he died at the age of eighty-eight, Wesley left behind a worn coat, a battered hat, a humble cottage, a tattered Bible, and the Methodist Church.

Pastor, when you die, what will you leave behind? I hope you will leave behind a strong, vibrant, dynamic congregation that will carry on the work of God for generations to come. If you do, it will be because you died to yourself as Wesley did and become a servant of God and of humanity. That is the way to lasting happiness. That is the way to true greatness. That is the way to grow an evangelistic church.

8
Work Smarter, Not Harder

Not long ago I was walking across the grounds of Glorieta Baptist Assembly with a group of preacher friends when one of them asked how many books I have written. When I told him, John Sullivan asked, "Who is your ghost writer?"

I responded, "The Holy Ghost."

Of course, neither of us was serious. But behind John's question was the problem of where we find time to do all that we need to do. This is a constant problem when you are trying to grow an evangelistic church.

This has always been a problem. When William Laud was appointed archbishop of Canterbury in 1633, he wrote: "There is more expected from me than the craziness of these times will give me leave to do." And Malcolm Forbes opined, "Unless you are serving time, there is never enough of it."

The secret to having enough time to do everything that needs to be done is found in the words on a sticker I have placed on the middle drawer of my desk. It says, "Work smarter, not harder."

There are several smart things that all of us can do to accomplish more.

Get a Good Secretary

There are many pastors who are deeply committed to the Lord's work, but who are bound by numerous tasks which they have never learned to delegate. The primary work of a pastor is to study God's Word and equip people for the ministry. A competent secretary can free you to do this and to extend your ministry as no one or nothing else can.

The first person a church acquires is usually the pastor. The second should be a secretary. If you are afraid you can't keep a secretary busy, relax! Your job isn't to make work for her but to let her make you more effective in your work.

If there are some things you just like to do your own way, and you have never been able to commit them a secretary, maybe you need to shake loose of that attitude in order to grow as a leader.

And if you think you can't afford a secretary, begin with a volunteer or a corps of volunteers. There are always ladies who will work for the Lord and His church in this way. They will fold and mail bulletins, answer the phone, type letters, assist with mailings, and perform many other necessary though mundane tasks.

As the church grows larger, it will be able to hire a full-time secretary. When that time comes, look for someone with a deep commitment to Christ, not someone who is just looking for a job. Acquire someone who is highly skilled, who has a stable home situation. This is a protection from transference of affection between two people who work closely together. In addition, the secretary "carries" the pastor. She is the "right hand" that supports him and frees him to minister. It would be counterproductive to reverse this situation, especially if she needed his constant counseling support to keep her going.

She should also be pleasant, loyal, able to keep confidences, cooperative, well organized, and dress in such a way as to represent Christ and His church well.

In a small church, the secretary does everything! She has to because she is the only one in the office. Daily chores will include phone and receptionist duties, preparing the bulletin, ordering supplies, duplicating papers for committees, taking dictation, and trying to keep the pastor on his schedule. Obviously, she must be versatile and able to work with interruptions.

In the large church a multiple secretarial staff serves together, and each has specialized duties.

My secretary, Gloria Ortega, has been with me for ten years. She is so efficient and such a valuable helper that in some ways she has become my assistant. She screens my calls, prepares hospital lists for me, makes my appointments, keeps my calendar, and occasionally writes letters for me.

She often ministers to hurting people over the phone or even in her own office: listening, counseling, and praying with them. She is a strong encourager to the church volunteers. And she represents me and the church as she deals with people.

She shares my ministry and thus frees me to concentrate on greater matters.

Work by a Schedule

Time is the raw material out of which our life and our ministry are fashioned. Our success, or a lack of it, will be largely contingent upon the effective use of time. Time is immensely valuable and utterly irretrievable. Yet despite its preciousness and vast potential, there is nothing we squander quite as thoughtlessly as time.

Time is especially easily wasted in church vocations. There are no set hours to work, no prescribed routines to follow, and no supervisors to help us. It is possible to be lazy and often get away with it.

The effective use of time demands perseverance and self-discipline. The management of time will be a lifelong process, but there is no investment that will pay higher dividends for you and for your church.

It will help if you will develop a routine to your work week as well as your work day. As a minister, you may not be able to maintain a rigid schedule, but you should have some type of pattern for your ministry.

Once you have developed your personal schedule, share it with the congregation. If the church understands the minister's schedule, they will respect it. We must always be available for emergencies, but people will be willing to give you time that you need for study and sermon preparation if they know what your schedule is.

My personal schedule is to reserve the mornings for study. During that period of time I try not to be available for anything except emergencies.

Phone calls are saved, and I return them between eleven and twelve. Then I usually have lunch with a prospect or a church member. My afternoons are used in the following ways:

Monday is administrative day. That morning I write the pastor's page of our church paper, plan my weekly schedule, and do general administrative work. At noon I have lunch with my staff followed by our weekly staff meeting. After staff meeting, I enjoy recreation with some of my staff members. Some jog, some bowl, and some play racketball.

Tuesday is pastoral ministry day. That afternoon I visit the hospitals, shut-ins, and members of my congregation who need a home visit.

Wednesday is counseling day. The whole afternoon is devoted to seeing people who have personal problems. Appointments are made through my secretary.

Thursday is study and writing day. I usually go out to a small lake house on the edge of town and spend both the morning and the afternoon in sermon preparation and writing projects.

Friday is catch-up day. I use that afternoon for additional study, visitation, or administration as needed.

Saturday is rest day. Except for weddings, funerals, and other occasional activities, I spend Saturdays working around the house.

Sunday is worship day.

As you would know I am not always able to maintain this rigid weekly and daily schedule, but it is at least a general framework for me to get the most done.

Manage Your Time Effectively

Experience proves that most time is wasted not in hours but in minutes. A bucket with a small hole in the bottom gets just as empty as a bucket that is deliberately kicked over. So effective time management is one of the keys to getting all the necessary things done.

Good time management requires personal discipline and constant vigilance. But it pays rich dividends. Time management is especially difficult for ministers because so much of their work relates to the needs and schedules of other people. Ministers are constantly subject to interruptions they cannot control.

Being in the people business, however, is no excuse for not trying to improve the management of time. On the contrary, improvement of time management will mean more people can be served more effectively.

I've struggled to find time-management practices that work for me. Here is my list of "top ten" suggestions.

1. Plan your work and work your plan. Making a weekly and a daily "to-do" list is perhaps the single most important time-management tool ever conceived. A list not only helps you remember what needs be done, it aids you in setting priorities for the day. Make a list and check off the important items first. It will give you a sense of satisfaction as you progress through the list. You may not complete the list, but you will have the satisfaction of knowing that you are tending to that which matters most for that day. It is important that you begin the next day by making a new list and setting your priorities for that day.

2. Use your prime time to handle the most important items.

Prime time is when you do your best work—maybe early in the morning, perhaps midafternoon, or late in the evening. Most people have certain periods of the day when they are most alert and most productive. It is vital to learn how to work with your body and not against it. Take advantage of those times in the day when you are most creative and build your schedule around it.

Other available time is best for attending to other people's needs—those with whom you relate in ministry. Don't spend your prime time on nonprime activities.

3. Group activities. Save up for a special time each day matters like returning telephone calls, seeing staff members, or writing letters.

4. Handle a piece of paper only once. Answer most letters right on the letter itself and return it to the sender. It is often easy to think of a reply when you have just read the letter, and your reaction is fresh on your mind. Occasionally, a decision will call for more thought, and you may have to put off a reply. But when possible, answer the letter immediately and forget about it.

5. Use odd moments well. A university analysis showed that the average individual spends three years of his or her lifetime just waiting. And a Gallup Poll which sampled one-hundred persons at random reported that every one of them expected to do some waiting during the next few hours, but only one out of eight had any plans for making constructive use of the time.

Put "waiting time" to good use. Relax, read, or do something else you wouldn't otherwise have done. Carry blank three-by-five index cards in your pocket to jot down notes and ideas. Have a book to read. Some of the world's great leaders have well used their waiting time. Robert Louis Stevenson seldom left home without two books in his pocket: one to read and one in which to jot down notes. William Lyon Phelps carried on a voluminous correspondence in the chinks of time between appointments.

None of us would think of throwing away the nickels and quarters and dimes that accumulate in our pockets. But almost all of us do throw away the small-change time—five minutes here, a quarter hour there—that accumulates in any ordinary day.

Learn to be a wait-watcher.

6. Use the Swiss cheese approach to cut a big job down to size. Identify small pieces of a big job that can be done when you have small segments of time between appointments. When you have fifteen minutes before meeting someone for lunch or for an appointment to arrive, you can make several calls or collect materials to get ready for the job you plan to do later.

Shoot a big job full of holes and it will go faster.

7. Control interruptions during study and writing. Each time a job is put down, a certain amount of start-up time is required to pick it up again. For study and writing to be most productive, a person needs periods of time without interruptions. Pick a time and place and stick to it.

8. Conduct stand-up conferences. It is a gracious gesture to invite someone to take a seat in your office. However, you can be sure that a small item of business will turn into a thirty-minute conference when you and your guest are seated. True, many extended conversations are valuable times of ministry. However, these conversations can also be time wasters if they do not have a specific purpose.

9. Learn to say no. It's easy to become overcommitted. When a person tries to be all things to all people, everything suffers. Knowing when and how to say no is a time-management skill that is hard to learn but one that pays big dividends.

10. Delegate whenever possible. Ask yourself, "Am I doing anything that could be done by someone other than me? Am

I doing something that could be done as well or even better by others?" If the answer is yes, then delegate it now.

Effective delegation involves selecting, training, supporting, and appreciating the efforts of others. If someone can do a job acceptably, involve him or her in doing it.

Effective delegation not only recognizes the gifts of others but also enables you to multiply yourself through others.

Remember that there is always enough time for the important matters—especially to fulfill God's purpose for our lives. It is futile to say, "I wish I had more time." We already have all the time we will get. The key is to use the time we have as effectively as possible.

Eat Well and Exercise

I am a goal-oriented person. So at the beginning of each year, I set goals for myself in all areas of life: physical, financial, professional, social, and spiritual. Physically, I want to keep my weight between 185 to 190 pounds. I run two miles three times a week for my cardiovascular system. I do one hundred sit-ups a day to keep my muscles in tone. And I eat well and rest adequately for my general health.

We make a lot of jokes about exercise. Jimmy Allen commented that he gets his exercise from serving as a pallbearer for his jogger friends. John Childs reports that he is a member of "Exercisers' Anonymous." "If you get an urge to jog, call us, and we will sit with you until it passes," he quips.

But all of us know that we work better and live longer if we care for our bodies, which are temples of the Holy Ghost.

Above all, learn to take time to do something that restores the zest to your life. Life is not a 100-yard dash but more of a cross-country run. If we sprint all the time, we may not only fail to win the race but never even last long enough to reach the finish line. So slow down long enough to rest adequately. John Ruskin observed, "There is no music in a 'rest'—but there's the making of music in it. And people are always missing that part of life's melody."

Outsiders are frequently unaware of the intensity of an average work week around a church, ranging from busy to chaotic. But we are. And the only way to get everything done that needs to be done is to work smarter, not harder. It's an absolute necessity if you want to grow an evangelistic church.

9
The Second Most Important Thing

One of Henry Kaiser's keys to success was working with other people. He believed that you seldom accomplish very much by yourself. So he was constantly seeking the opinions of others and drawing around him the most capable assistants possible.

"I make progress," wrote the late and great industralist, "by having people around me who are smarter than I am—and listening to them. And I assume that everyone is smarter about something than I am."

Working well with others is not only one of the keys to success in industry, it is also a key to success in the work of God.

A law of church growth is: to the degree that we will not share our ministry with others, we limit our growth. After all, one person can only do so much. I know of a very capable pastor whose church is in a prime location in a growing city who is doing this right now. For some reason he refuses to add staff to his church and share his ministry with them. I don't know why he is like that. It may be due to past staff problems. It is more likely that he is insecure and wants to control everything himself. For whatever the reason, his church has failed to reach its potential because he has not expanded himself through a shared ministry.

The person in a place of leadership who fails to share his

ministry through delegation is constantly enmeshed in a morass of secondary details that not only overburden him but deflect him from primary responsibilities, and he also fails to release the leadership potential of those under his authority. To insist on doing things oneself because it will be done better is not only a short-sighted policy but may be evidence of an unwarranted conceit.

The outstanding biblical illustration of the importance of a shared ministry is that of Jethro's advice to his son-in-law Moses (Ex. 18:1-27).

Israel had emerged from Egypt an unorganized horde of slaves. By that time a new national spirit was developing, and they were becoming an organized nation. The intolerable administrative burdens which that imposed on Moses sparked Jethro's sound advice. From morning till night he saw Moses hearing and adjudicating the endless problems arising from these new conditions. Moses was saddled with both legislative and judicial functions, and his decisions were accepted by the people as the oracles of God.

Jethro saw that Moses could not indefinitely endure the strain and advanced two strong reasons in favor of delegation of some of his responsibilities. First, "You will surely wear out, . . . for the task is too heavy for you; you cannot do it alone" (v. 18, NASB). There are limits to the expenditure of physical and nervous force beyond which it is not safe to go. Second, the present method was too slow, and the people were becoming dissatisfied because they were not receiving the attention they desired. Sharing responsibility would speed up legal decisions, and the people would go away satisfied.

Jethro then proposed a twofold course of action. Moses should continue to act as God's representative, teaching spiritual principles and exercising his legislative functions. It would be for him to bring the hard cases to God. He should delegate the judicial functions that he had hitherto exercised to competent legal officers who could thus lighten his intolerable burden. It was wise advice, and fortunately Moses was not too proud to recognize the wisdom in it and act upon it. Had Moses succumbed to the strain of his office, he would have left behind him no one experienced and trained in exercising authority and bearing responsibility. Failure to make such provision has spelled ruin to many a promising work of God.

Jethro's suggested standards of selection of helpers for Moses evidenced true spiritual discernment. They had to be men of ability, for theirs would be an exacting task; they had to be men of piety who feared God and respected their fellowmen, and they had to be men of honor who hated covetousness and would not be susceptible to bribery.

Jethro encouraged Moses by stating a spiritual principle of timeless relevance. "If you do this thing and God so commands you, then you will be able to endure" (Ex. 18:23, NASB).

The principle is that God assumes full responsibility for enabling His people to fulfill every task to which He has appointed them. There are some self-imposed tasks that others can do better than we can, and we should relinquish them. But even should they do them worse, we should still relinquish them: a severe test for the perfectionist! Moses could doubtless have done the task better than the seventy men whom he selected, but had he persisted in doing so, Moses would soon have been only a memory.

Several benefits accrued to Moses through Jethro's advice. He was able to concentrate on the higher aspects and responsibilities of his office. The latent and unsuspected talents of many of his subordinates were discovered. Those gifted men, who might have become his critics had he continued to keep things in his own hands, were developed by the burden of their office and became his staunch allies. And the disaffection of the people was stifled by the speeding up of legal processes. He also made provision for the effective leadership of the nation after his death.

There is a lesson here for modern leaders. It is a mistake to assume more duties than we can adequately and satisfactorily discharge. There is no virtue in doing more than our fair share of the work. It is good to be able to recognize and accept our own limitations. Our Jethros can often discern, more clearly than we can the cost at which our leadership is being exercised, and we would be wise to heed their admonitions. If we break natural law, even in the service of God, we are not exempted from its penalties.

Jesus, too, saw the need of a shared ministry. After a busy day of preaching, teaching, and healing, He was overwhelmed by the needs of the multitudes. So He said to His disciples, "The harvest truly is plenteous, but the labourers are few; Pray ye therefore the Lord of harvest, that he will send forth labourers into his harvest" (Matt. 9:37-38).

If Jesus felt the need of having others share His ministry, to make it more effective, surely we have the same need.

The apostles, as we shall see in more detail in a later chapter, were soon to learn the same lesson. By the time of Acts 6, the membership of the young church had multiplied so rapidly that the apostles were not able to preach, pray, and adequately administer the benevolent work of the church at the same time. The result was that some widows were neglected in ministry and had begun to complain. Multiplication without ministry always leads to murmuring. So they expanded themselves by leading the church to ordain seven deacons to direct its benevolent ministry. In the same way, it is only as we expand ourselves through others that the work of God can be done adequately in our day.

Three factors are necessary for a shared ministry: first, the pastor must be secure enough not to be threatened by others. Second, the pastor must trust the abilities of others enough to give them the authority to act. And third, the pastor must be flexible enough to accept things not being done his way all the time.

Learning the Hard Way

Second only to a pastor's relationship to his people and his preaching is his relationship to his staff in growing an evangelistic church. If the pastor does not love and serve the people, they will not listen to him or follow him. If the pastor does not maintain good staff relations, then division will occur in the congregation, and it will dissipate its best energy on infighting. I learned that the hard way. There was a time when, because of several bad staff experiences, I actually doubted my ability to work closely with other people. This was due partly to my judgment and partly to my temperament. When I was about to move from one of my early pastorates, one of the good laypersons of the church advised me, "Paul, if you ever get out of the ministry, please don't go into personnel work because you sure don't know how to pick 'em." Poor picking was part of my problem.

But the biggest problem was my temperament. Like Moses I had an inferiority complex. People with inferiority complexes tend to one of two extremes. They either withdraw in timidity, or they become overly aggressive trying to prove their own worth to themselves. In my case, I became a workaholic. I drove myself unmercifully, and I expected the same kind of effort out of others. When they didn't give it, then I became dissatisfied.

I had actually earned a pretty nasty reputation. When Dennis Parrott, my present minister of education, was considering joining me twelve years ago, a friend advised him not to. He was afraid that Dennis would be hurt like some others had been. I don't think there was anything malicious in the friend's advice. He simply loved Dennis and knew my track record.

Fortunately, through the years I have learned to be more tolerant, less demanding, and easier to please. I suppose most of it is due to the mellowing of age, and some of it to the work of grace in my life. But a part of it has come from the realization that to grow an evangelistic church we must have a shared ministry.

Today I have a staff of ten men who share the ministry with me. Like the band of men that followed King Saul, they are "men whose hearts God had touched" (1 Sam. 10:26). We share both the responsibilities and the rewards of the ministry. Each person visits the hospitals, reads the Scripture, leads in prayer in public worship, and baptizes on a rotating basis. Each staff member shares in outreach and evangelistic visitation on a weekly basis. And each person shares in the thrill of victory and the agony of defeat. We are a team in every sense of the word.

The Key Man

The key to our good staff relations is Dennis Parrott, my minister of administration-education. The way Dennis and I began working together is a story all in itself. I was looking for my third minister of education in six years when Dennis was recommended to me. When I met Dennis, I was immediately impressed with him and asked him to join our staff. But Dennis didn't see the potential in that church that I saw, so he declined.

Not many months later, the pulpit committee of Green Acres Church invited me to preach in view of a call. I preached for them on Sunday morning, and the church voted to call me as pastor that night. When the chairman of the committee phoned to tell me the vote, I was undecided about what to do. So I asked for a week to think and pray. A week passed, and I was still undecided. I asked for an additional week. Again no clear direction came from God. Finally, one day, I picked up the phone and called Dennis. I explained, "Dennis, the Green Acres Church in Tyler has called me to be their pastor. I'll go if you'll go with me." Dennis had been talking with another church about joining their staff and was at the point of accepting their invitation when my call came. But without hesitation, he replied, "I'll go." After that I didn't have any choice.

I accepted the call to the church with the understanding that Dennis would be invited as minister of education. Within a month Dennis and his family joined us in Tyler.

We Are Different

Dennis and I are different in many ways. We differ in temperament. I am a dreamer; he is an implementer. I am an architect; he is an engineer. I'm an idealist; he is a realist.

I tend toward being an egotist. I think, *Everybody out there loves us. Why wouldn't they?* Dennis is more cautious. He keeps saying, "Watch out, there is somebody around the next corner who is out to get us." Together we make a good team. We work with optimistic caution.

When we began working together, we were also different in philosophy. Twelve years ago I would have done almost anything to build a Sunday School. I would have had dancing bears, clowns, Hollywood personalities, and a general circus atmosphere, if necessary, to induce the people to come to church. Dennis taught me that the best way to grow an evangelistic church was through a strong Sunday School. That has saved me from much foolishness and shallowness in my ministry. That's one of the ways Dennis has helped me the most.

While we differed in temperament and philosophy from the first, Dennis and I agreed theologically. When choosing a staff person to work with, you had better be sure of that person's theology. People can change their philosophy easier than they will change their theology.

A Growing Relationship

Good staff relations, like good marriages, take time to develop. When Dennis joined our staff, it was only as minister of education; I was the administrator. But as the church grew and the demands on my time increased, I realized that Dennis's gifts and temperament were more suited for administration than mine. So, gradually, I asked Dennis to take over the administrative responsibilities. This was not easy for me at first. My leadership style was a cross between Adolf Hitler and Joseph Stalin. I had run things for almost twenty years, and Dennis was ten years younger than I. It took time to complete the shift.

On several occasions I would give a responsibility to Dennis and then take it back again. Once we were planning an all-church picnic, and I outlined what I wanted done and asked Dennis to handle it. He accepted the responsibility. A day or two later, without saying anything to Dennis, I enlisted a lady to be the lay-director of the picnic. When Dennis heard about this, he came to my office and asked, "Do you want me to run this picnic or not?" I answered, "I sure do." He replied, "Then leave me alone and stop interfering, and I will get it done."

It took me a while to let go, but gradually I learned that if I would do the dreaming and let him do the implementing it would be better for everybody. He could be trusted, so I adjusted.

No Power Structure

One of the reasons Dennis and I have gotten along so well is that he has a servant's heart. He doesn't want to be pastor of the church. He wants to help me.

A lot of staff problems arise as a result of power struggles. You can't have two authorities. Somebody has to have the last word. Unless that is clear in everybody's mind, problems are inevitable.

Bart Starr, the former quarterback and later coach of the Green Bay Packers, was describing to a group of businessmen how his coach, Vince Lombardi, held absolute power. He stated that as you entered Vince's office, you noticed a huge mahogany desk with an impressive organizational chart behind it on the wall. The chart had a small block at the top in which was written: "Vince Lombardi, head coach and general manager." A line came down from it to a very large block on to which was printed, "Everybody else."

While I don't recommend that as the organizational chart for a church, ultimately and finally somebody has to be at the top and everybody else has to recognize and accept that fact. In any movement, among any people, somebody must be in charge. I am in charge, and Dennis graciously accepts that.

Dennis has plenty of authority in our church. We recently completed a new adult educational building. It cost $1.5 million and will house twelve hundred in Sunday School. Dennis was in charge of the project from beginning to end. He worked with the plans and survey committee, architects, and building committee to make every single decision involved. I did not make one decision concerning the entire building. He and the building committee picked the architect, chose the location, determined the size and design of the building, and selected the furniture. All I did was raise the money. That set me free to preach and pray, counsel, and visit as God called me to do, and as I like to do.

Several years ago, the minister of education of one of our leading churches in Texas was fired. Dennis knew the man and was aware that the minister had been assuming too much authority in the church. So Dennis came to me and said, "Paul, if you ever feel that I'm taking too much authority, just tell me so. I don't want what happened to my friend to happen to me."

After twelve years together, Dennis and I know each other so well that we can almost anticipate what the other is thinking or how one of us will react. He knows what to check with me on and is careful not to abuse his authority. He accepts the fact that the last word is mine.

Ready, Fire, Aim

One of the "burrs" Dennis has had to adjust to is my impulsiveness. In the book *The Pursuit of Excellence,* the author summed up the management of philosophy of one executive as: "Ready, fire, aim!" That's the way I am. I often shoot first and aim later.

One Sunday morning I announced to the congregation that on Promotion Day, October 1, we were going to have three thousand in Sunday School. We were averaging about eighteen hundred at the time, and that was quite a challenge. While I had thought about these plans for awhile, I had never discussed them with Dennis. One reason was: I knew Dennis would have wanted to set a more realistic goal—like twenty-three hundred—and would have probably talked me out of my goal. Dennis can talk me out of almost anything. So when I made my announcement from the pulpit that morning, that was the first Dennis knew of it. But after he regained consciousness, Dennis went to work to achieve the goal, and the end result was the largest Sunday School attendance in the history of our church: 2770.

Where We Are Now

Needless to note, through the years Dennis and I have both had our accusers and our antagonists. But Dennis defends me, and I defend him. He is a trusted friend, a counselor, an advisor, and a fellow laborer.

This feeling of trust, of loyalty, of closeness exists among all our staff. We really like one another. We have built and maintained this unity in several ways.

We begin with apt job descriptions and a good understanding

about our work before a person joins our staff. We don't try to court would-be staff people to get them to join us and then surprise them when the honeymoon is over.

We recently interviewed a prospective staff member who had been spending a lot of time on the golf course at his present church. When we were through, the man said to Dennis, "You guys really expect a person to work around here, don't you?" We are always up front about what we will do, how we work, and what we expect.

We have two staff retreats each year. The first, held in the spring, is a dreaming time. I ask everyone to pull out all the stops and share what they'd like to do in their area if they had unlimited finances and personnel. Then the whole staff is free to ask questions, make comments, and evaluate what has been proposed.

The second retreat, held in late summer, is for calendar planning. We take the best of what was proposed in the spring and distill it down to specific programs and dates. This becomes our calendar of activities for the next year.

Every Monday our staff has lunch together. After a time of informal fellowship over a meal, we have our staff meeting. We begin by reviewing last week's record: Sunday School attendance, giving, additions, staff visits, and so forth, and making staff visitation and ministry assignments for the coming week.

Then we circle the group and ask each person to share the highlights of his programs for the week and to present any problem we need to discuss.

We close the meeting on our knees in prayer for one another, the activities of the week, and the special needs of our people.

After staff meeting is over, we have recreation time. We not only plan together and pray together, we also play together. Some of our people jog, some bowl, and others play racketball.

Beyond that, Dennis and I maintain our open-door policy to

all the staff at all times. And it is not an open door to a closed mind. We listen and are ready to help however we can.

All of this together has created a real brotherhood among us that we feel has contributed to our growth as an evangelistic church. After all, how can we convince the world that we serve a God of love if we do not love and get along with one another?

The psalmist exulted, "Behold, how good and how pleasant it is for brethren to dwell together in unity!" (Ps. 133:1). I agree. Unity is good and pleasant, and it is a key to growing the kind of evangelistic church that wins and holds converts.

10
"A Few Good Funerals"

My busy afternoon was interrupted by the ringing of the telephone. On the other end of the line was a distraught church secretary I had known and loved since I was a child. She was calling to tell me that the church had just lost its pastor: the third one in five years. The secretary's analysis of the situation was that it was the deacons' fault. She cried, "They won't let the pastor lead the church, and they can't lead it." The result was disagreement, dissatisfaction, and division. So the pastor had left.

Then she blurted out, "What our church needs is a few good funerals."

I've been around long enough to know that the secretary's proposed solution was not the answer to their problem. Deacons (or elders or stewards, etc.) with the attitude, "We're supposed to run the church," have a way of perpetuating themselves. By the time one generation dies off, they have raised up another exactly like themselves to take their places.

The answer to this problem is not to be found in the cemetery, however, but in the Scriptures. What those deacons need, and what our churches need, is to be taught in a loving and helpful way that it is God's plan for His church to be led by a shepherd, not run by a board. The biblical pattern is for the pastor to lead the flock and for the deacons and staff to share the ministry with the pastor. An understanding of the meaning

of the word *deacon* and the origin of the office of deacon is a
good place to start. The word *deacon* literally means "servant."
The biblical account of the choosing of the first deacons makes
it clear that deacons were never intended to "run the church"
but rather to serve the church. They were first set aside to share
in the ministry with the apostles.

An understanding and a practice of this shared-ministry concept is another one of the secrets to growing an evangelistic
church. The happiest and healthiest churches I know are those
where the ministry of the church is shared not only by the staff
but also by the deacons.

This concept of a shared ministry is made clear in the scriptural account of the choosing of the first deacons in Acts 6.
When the church came into being on the day of Pentecost, the
apostles began immediately to preach and practice all that they
had learned from Jesus. This involved meeting human needs as
well as proclaiming divine truth.

One fact the apostles remembered about Jesus was the money
bag that Judas had kept for Him. Funds from it were often used
to help the poor (John 13:29). So the apostles opened their
purses to help the poor also, and they led the church to establish
a benevolent ministry. All was going well until there was a
failure of structure. An effective ministry was advancing so
swiftly that no one had kept pace with the practicalities of
administration.

You can trace the problem. Acts 2 shows the explosion of
sharing and caring, a result of the joy of knowing Christ as Lord
and Messiah. Those with material resources were glad to give
to those in need. This ad-hoc generosity, however, could only
last so long before someone would misuse it. At some point, a
few perceptive people must have come to the apostles and
suggested that financial help be channeled and directed for
maximum impact and fairness.

"Perhaps," I imagine someone remarked, "they'll know how to distribute it fairly to the disadvantaged."

Something like that must have happened, because in Acts 4:37 we are told the money for charitable purposes was laid at the apostles' feet. How long did this system work? Who knows? One truth is certain: by Acts 6 the new system was breaking down. Too many things were slipping through administrative cracks. The results? An unhappy, complaining congregation.

Granted, the people shouldn't have complained, at least not the way the dissidents in Jerusalem were doing. But we must also admit that a new organizational system was needed, one that would meet the need and set everyone free to concentrate on ministry. Thus, the Jerusalem church reorganized! The results were healthier relationships, effective distribution to the needy, and further expansion of the congregation itself.

The apostles led out. They suggested that the congregation choose seven reputable, wise, and Spirit-filled men "whom we may appoint over this business" (Acts 6:3). The church responded, and that was the beginning of the office of deacon.

Some people, reading that King James phrase "over this business," have argued, "See, deacons were chosen to be over the business of the church." I agree so long as we realize what the real "business" of the church is. *It is ministry.* These first deacons were chosen to administer the benevolent work of the church in a fair and equitable manner and to thus free the apostles, devoting themselves to preaching and praying as the Lord intended. This would be a shared ministry at its best. When they did this, the divided church was reunited, and another period of rapid growth followed.

In this biblical account, there are at least three principles that provide a foundation for a shared ministry and for growing an evangelistic church today.

A Better Division of Labor

The first principle is this: the pastor is not to do all the work of the church; the pastor is to see that all the work is done. That is a new and revolutionary concept to some churches and even to some pastors. But it is at the heart of the biblical teaching about a ministering church.

The apostle Paul declared that the ascended Lord had given to His church certain gifted leaders, among them pastors, to equip the saints to do the work of the ministry and to build up His body (Eph. 4:11-12). It is clearly the intent of God that the work of the ministry be done by all the church and that the pastor be the one who trains and supervises them.

There are three words used interchangeably in the New Testament for the one office of pastor. They are the words *shepherd, elder,* and *bishop.* The word *bishop* means "overseer" or "superintendent."

We have had so many building programs in our church in the past ten years that one of our people said we should change the name of our fund-raising efforts from "Together We Build" to "Forever We Build"! In each of those major building programs, the contractor had a building superintendent to oversee the construction project. I have observed that those building superintendents did not do all of the work on the buildings. They saw to it that it was all done. They didn't lay any of the bricks; yet they saw to it that the bricks were laid. They didn't install the plumbing; they made sure that it was installed. They didn't paint the walls; they saw that the walls were painted.

It is the job of a construction superintendent to have the right workers on the job at the right time and to see that they do their work correctly. If superintendents tried to do all the work themselves, they would have to be skilled workers in every trade, and the projects would never be completed. But by using the skills of various building trades people and having the right workers at the right place at the right time, the project went forward with speed and effectiveness.

It is to be the same in churches. The use of the word *bishop* for the office of pastor suggests that the pastor is to be an overseer, a superintendent of God's work. Pastors are not to do all the work. They are to see that all the work is done. It is their job to enlist, equip, assign, and inspire the people to do the work of God.

Our churches today need a better division of labor. Most church staffs are both overworked and underemployed. They are overworked at a hundred little things and underemployed at the basic calling to train and equip the people for the work of the ministry.

While the prophet Jonah was swallowed by a whale, today's modern-day prophet is nibbled to death by a thousand minnows of interruptions. The solution: let the pastor be a superintendent, an overseer, and spread the work of the ministry among all the members of the church, especially the deacons.

The Primary Qualifications

The second principle of a ministering church is: when people are filled with the Holy Spirit, they are basically equipped to minister. The qualifications for the first deacons were simple. They were to be men with good reputations, sound judgment, and *full of the Holy Ghost.*

If these men were to be out among the people hearing their complaints, discerning their needs, and dispensing financial aid fairly, then they would have to be men who were highly respected and who exercised good judgment. Being filled with the Holy Spirit would equip them and energize them to do the work of God effectively. The Holy Spirit who came at Pentecost comes to dwell in us the moment we put our faith and trust in Jesus Christ. He endows all believers with one or more spiritual gifts so they may minister in some way to the body of Christ on earth—the church (1 Cor. 12:1-31; Rom. 12:3-38; Eph. 4:7-13).

Someone has observed memorably that God has chosen to dwell in four places: His *prior* house was the first person, Adam. God breathed into Adam the breath of life, the Spirit; that was God's prior house.

After that, God's *provisional* house was the tabernacle and the Temple in the Old Testament. God chose to dwell in that tent and in that pile of stones.

God's *perfect* house was the Lord Jesus Christ. He had the Spirit of God without measure.

God's *permanent* house is the individual believer and that collection of believers called *the church.*

In the Old Testament God had a Temple for His people. In the New Testament, God has a people for His temple. Paul declared in 1 and 2 Corinthians that we are the temple of the Spirit of God. Individually and collectively, we are the dwelling place of God. The moment we receive the Savior, the Holy Spirit takes up residence inside us.

It is His power that equips us and empowers us for effective service. He has all that is needed. We have all that He is. That is all it takes. Or, as a converted prostitute and drug addict put it, "He put unction in my gumption, so I could function."

The Holy Spirit is looking for someone to work through. It is the clear teaching of Scripture that when average Christians, the plain vanilla church members, furnish the Holy Spirit a body—hands, feet, eyes, lips—He will then use them effectively in God's service.

How Big Should a Church Be?

This experience has a happy ending. As a result of the apostles' and the deacons' sharing the ministry of the church, another growth spiral resulted. Luke recorded, "The word of God increased; and the number of the disciples multiplied in Jerusalem greatly; and a great company of priests were obedient to the faith" (Acts 6:7). This suggests the third principle of a ministering church: a ministering church will be a happy church, and a happy church will be a growing church.

How big should a church be? From a study of Acts, there is apparently no limit to how large a church can be so long as it can maintain a personal ministry to all of its members. Its size is to be limited only by the number of active, dedicated lay ministers it has.

I once thought that a church should not be larger than three- or four-hundred members. But I was thinking only in terms of the number of people I could personally visit regularly and counsel effectively. Then, as I studied the Book of Acts, I realized that my idea was not scriptural. Obviously, God intended His church to be very big. It started small, with only the twelve apostles for the first three years. Then on the Day of Pentecost alone, three thousand members were added to it (Acts 2:41). Following Pentecost, the Lord added to the church daily those who were being saved.

A short while later at a Temple service, five thousand people were saved (Acts 4:4). After the deaths of Ananias and Sapphira a multitude of believers, both men and women, were added to the Lord (Acts 5:14). And then comes verse 1 in Acts 6 telling that the number of the disciples multiplied greatly in Jerusalem.

When I read the Book of Acts, I leave it with the feeling that our churches today are not thinking big enough. We are not as growth conscious as we ought to be. We may not be placing as much emphasis on numbers as we should. We are thinking and talking of hundreds when we should be thinking and talking of thousands. We talk of addition when we ought to be praying for multiplication. We might need a refresher course in divine mathematics.

God's plan seems clear to me: He expects His church to be

a growing and a ministering church, to become larger and larger, but to maintain a personal touch all the while. The deacons are to be the primary means of the church's maintaining this personal ministry while it continues to grow.

When pastors pray and preach and when deacons minister, the church has an unbeatable combination for doing both. These held in balance will create peace and harmony among God's people and enable us to grow an evangelistic church that reaches and keeps people.

11
Look for the Gold

Leaders may map out their campaigns with the greatest of care; they may choose their sphere of operation, their time and place of attack with the greatest of skill and insight, but ultimately they are dependent on their people for success. "One man," stated Field Marshal Montgomery, "can lose me a battle." Unless leaders have people on whom they can rely to accept their orders and to carry out their plans, all their wisdom and foresight can go to nothing.

Douglas Blatherwick, in *A Layman Speaks,* tells how, in Champness Hall in Rochdale, there was a concert by the Halle Orchestra under Sir John Barbirolli. The hall was crowded to capacity. As the crowd was leaving the hall, a man said to the minister: "When are you going to have this place full on a Sunday evening?" The minister answered, "I shall have this place full on a Sunday evening when, like Sir John Barbirolli, I have under me eighty trained and disciplined men." Anyone leading a campaign must have a staff through whom he can act.

That was true of Jesus. If His work was to go on, He had to gather around Him an inner circle of men whom He could train to know Him, to understand Him, to love Him, and who would come to know His purpose and His task. He had to have men who would carry on His work when He had to leave the world in the body. So the time came when Jesus chose the men who were to be His twelve apostles (Matt. 10:1). For Him, His men had to be the living books on which He imprinted His message.

Later He would reach out in an even wider circle to choose seventy others whom He would train to share in His great mission in the same way (Luke 10:1).

To grow an evangelistic church, you need a shared ministry that reaches beyond the staff and even the deacons. It needs to include as many laypersons as possible.

Overlook the Dirt

But where do we find men like Jesus found? Andrew Carnegie once had thirty millionaires working for him. That's when a million dollars was a million dollars. Someone asked Carnegie how he induced that many millionaires to work for him. He replied that they weren't millionaires when he hired them; they made it while they were with him.

"How do you find such men?" they inquired. He answered, "It's like mining for gold. When you start you may have to move tons of dirt to find a gold nugget, . . . but when you start mining for gold, you overlook the dirt."

We need to look for gold in the lives of others. That's what Jesus did. He found fishermen, government tax employees, political extremists—regular folks—and He brought out the best in them. We must do the same.

Let me tell you about one such man. Five years ago, Charles Moore, one of my best friends, expressed concern about a friend of his who was not a Christian. He said to me at dinner one night, "I sure wish we could get Joe Barentine to come to church." Then almost in the same breath Charles remarked, "But there is no way we could ever get Joe in a church house."

I suggested that Charles try to put Joe and me together in an informal meeting sometime. A few weeks later we were having a men's fish fry at our lake property, so Charles invited Joe and me to be his guests. During the evening I had an opportunity to be alone with Joe, and I invited him to church. To the surprise of everyone—including me—he showed up the following Sunday.

Up until that time Joe's whole life had centered around his work. He had been a home builder and a developer and had made enough money to live on. So he had decided to retire at fifty-nine. This change in Joe's life, plus serving on the jury of a gruesome sex-mutilation murder trial at about the same time, had changed his whole outlook on life and had made him open to the gospel.

There is a lesson in this for all of us. The fact that persons are not interested in Christ or His church today does not necessarily mean that they will not be interested tomorrow.

So don't ever write anybody off as hopeless.

Joe started coming to church every Sunday. But he still needed a new challenge in life. He needed something to give his life meaning. I had an idea. So, one day, I invited Joe to lunch and outlined my dreams for building a retreat center. Our church had owned eighteen acres of beautiful timberland on a lake not far from Tyler, but nothing had been done to develop it. It was just like it had been since God created it. After sharing with Joe my dreams for a lodge, a dormitory, and two cabins, I asked him if he would build them for us without cost. We would provide the materials and some of the labor: he would do the rest—all free!

Surprise number two, Joe said yes. For the next year, Joe worked full-time building our retreat center. He cleared the land, poured the concrete slabs, welded and erected the steel, and did virtually everything else by himself. What he couldn't do by himself, and we couldn't do by volunteer help, he contracted. The end result was one of the most beautiful retreat centers any church could want, and all at a fraction of what it would have cost otherwise.

Just as Joe completed the retreat center our church made a

commitment to help our missionaries evangelize Belize, Central America. It was a faith commitment because we had no funds available. We would build up to twenty church buildings in the next five years, put a Bible in the hands of every person in the country, help train the national Christian leadership, conduct evangelistic crusades and Bible schools, and do medical missions. We had already bought a small farm that would be used as a national retreat-conference center and a base of operations for our missionary teams. The retreat center needed a tabernacle, dormitories, and a caretaker's cottage built on it. And the construction of work buildings would require expert supervision. Other lay people had been enlisted for the other areas of work, but the construction programs would be the most difficult to carry out. They would require months of being away from home in a foreign country and working under extremely difficult circumstances. We would need a real expert to handle that. I asked Joe to do it. His response was less than enthusiastic. He did, however, at my insistence, agree to make a trip to Belize with Charles to evaluate the work. The day following his return from Belize Joe came to see me. He sat down in my office and tersely said, "I hate you."

I asked, flustered, "What do you mean, Joe?"

He came back, "You knew exactly what would happen. I have never felt more at home anywhere in all of my life than I did in Belize. The minute I stepped off the plane I knew that I belonged there."

Then, with tears in his eyes, "I will give you the next five years of my life. I will build those buildings."

Spared for a Purpose

Then Joe told me the following stories: in the summer of 1941 he was driving a truck in California when he learned that our government was looking for construction workers for several overseas projects. So he applied for a job. They gave Joe his choice of working in one of three locations: Alaska, Panama, or a tiny island in the South Pacific called Wake Island. Joe didn't want to be in the mosquitoes of Panama or the cold of Alaska, so he chose Wake Island. He got all of his papers ready and then discovered that he had to have a birth certificate before he could be accepted. He wrote home and asked that it be sent. All he needed to do was to show up at the pier in Oakland with his clothes and birth certificate on the day of departure. The Friday the ship was to sail came and went, and to his disappointment his birth certificate had not arrived. Friday evening at 6:00 PM the ship sailed without him.

The next morning Joe dropped by the post office to check and see if he had any mail. His birth certificate was in his post office box. He told the postal clerk about his disappointment that the certificate had arrived too late for him to catch the ship to Wake Island. She told him that the birth certificate had arrived in plenty of time, but it had been placed in the wrong postal box. They had discovered the error the night before and only that morning had put it into his box.

The ship that Joe was to catch sailed to Wake Island and was docked there when the island was attacked by the Japanese. The ship was destroyed, and everyone on board was killed. Had Joe's birth certificate arrived on time, he would have sailed to a certain death.

He had a second brush with death in the fall of 1953. He was flying an Erecoupe plane, the first jet plane to be flown in the United States, and was coming in for a landing at the airport in Hurly, New Mexico. It was nighttime and neither Joe nor his copilot saw a large power line that stretched across the end of the runway. The plane hit the power line in such a way that it snapped like a violin string and sent fire shooting everywhere. If they had been flying six inches higher, the wire would have caught the landing gear and flipped it into a certain crash. If they had been flying six inches lower, the wire would have slid across the top of the plane and sheared the plastic canopy—and their heads—off. By some miracle, however, the plane hit the wire in the exact center of the one twelve-inch span where it could without killing them.

Joe's problems were not over, however, because the power line had shorted out all the lights in the airport, and they were forced to land in the blackness of the night with no runway or tower lights at all.

These were two brushes with death that Joe had miraculously survived by what he believed to be divine intervention.

Then Joe confessed, "I've always wondered why God spared my life. Now I know. I was left here to build those churches in Belize. I will take on the challenge."

In the last three years Joe has made over twenty trips to Belize and has built the tabernacle, dormitory, and caretaker's house we needed at the retreat center and has overseen the construction of a beautiful church in the capital city of Belmopan and another church in the village of Hattieville.

They Prayed for Thirteen Years

Recently, when I went to Belize to dedicate those two buildings, I learned that some of the people in Hattieville had been praying for thirteen years that they might one day have a church in their village. It was thrilling to see the answer to their prayer made possible by the work of a "pure-gold" layman.

The work in Belize has just begun, and Joe is right in the middle of it. You don't find men like Joe every day, but they are out there if you will look for the gold, not for the dirt.

How do you enlist them? How do you get laypersons involved? There is no substitute for asking them face-to-face, one-on-one. That's how Jesus did it. He didn't make a public appeal for apostles. He didn't wait for volunteers. He saw the men He wanted and enlisted them individually. You can best do it the same way.

Look around you and find people who are capable, dedicated, and teachable, and ask them to meet with you once a week for breakfast or lunch and Bible study. Take them visiting with you. Ask them to accompany you when you travel to one-night speaking engagements in other churches. Let them give their testimonies in worship services. They will catch your spirit and learn from you just as the apostles did from Jesus. That's the way to enlist laypersons anytime, anywhere, and for any cause.

Why Are They So Important?

The more you enlist, train, and motivate laypersons, the more you will deepen their dedication, broaden your effectiveness, and the more the church will come alive.

I read once of a flock of crows who disputed possession of a cornfield with a farmer and his sons. Again and again, they returned to the attack. But at last a shower of buckshot sent them flying in terror. Assembling gloomily on the edge of the woods, they held a council of war. One young and vigorous crow rose and thrust out his chest. "As far as I can see," he said, "there are more crows than men, and we can fly which men cannot. So why do we not assemble and destroy these creatures who presume to govern us and drive us from our food? Then we could eat all the corn we want, and there would be no one to stop us." An older crow at the edge of the flock interrupted. "That is all very well," he said, "but in my lifetime I have observed this one thing: where there are no men, there are also no cornfields."

It is the same in the spiritual realm. Where there are no laypersons sowing and reaping, the harvest is meager, and the church is dead.

To grow an evangelistic church, enlist laypersons, and share your ministry with them. That's the way to win and hold converts.

12
In Pursuit of Excellence

Bishop Keyes once wrote, "We need to recover and maintain a balance between a 'red-hot evangelism' and a 'down-to-earth' religious education."

A red-hot evangelism is our lifeblood, our calling. No one questions that. But we also need a "down-to-earth" religious education. Most of our churches need to take off the rose-colored glasses and admit that they have spawned a generation of biblical illiterates. Our churches are filled with people who have no idea what they believe or why they believe it. We have rocked ourselves to sleep with the illusion that we can stroll into a Sunday School classroom with a quarter in one hand and a quarterly in the other and teach people effectively all the things that Jesus commanded us.

We have settled for a mediocrity in our Bible-teaching program that is both a menace and a malignancy. It is high time that we stop muddling along and begin to pursue excellence in the religious-education program of our churches. This is an absolute essential for anyone who wants to grow an evangelistic church.

We need the commitment to excellence expressed by the apostle Paul, "I count not myself to have apprehended: but this one thing I do, forgetting those things which are behind, and reaching forth unto those things which are before, I press toward the mark for the prize of the high calling of God in Christ Jesus" (Phil. 3:13-14).

The apostle Paul never felt that he had arrived in his Christian life. He was always striving, always growing, always becoming. So should we.

A couple of years ago I was in Central Texas for a church-growth conference. Throughout the day I talked about the importance of vision, faith, enthusiasm, and hard work in church growth. At the close of the day an elderly lady named Lillian Burnsides said to me, "Now, maybe I can go back home and become a better Woman's Missionary Union president." Later I found out that Miss Lillian was ninety-three years old. Think of that: ninety-three and still serving and growing. That's the way we should all be.

A commitment to excellence involves a commitment to the basics of Christian education. If we master the basics, the rest will come naturally. Ron Proctor, a fellow Christian worker, told me that he once met Bob Lilly, the former all-pro tackle of the Dallas Cowboys, in a Dallas shopping center. Bob Lilly, who is now a Christian, may be the greatest defensive tackle ever to play professional football. He began playing as a seventh grader in junior high school and then eventually reached the ultimate in professional sports, an all-pro performer. As they discussed Bob's career that day Ron asked, "Bob, you have played football at every level of competition from junior high to all-pro status. What's the difference in playing football in the seventh grade and as a professional?"

Bob Lilly replied, "Really, not that much. In the seventh grade we learned to punt, pass, and kick! Run, block, and tackle! And we still do essentially the same things as a pro. The difference is that we learn to master the basics."

That's the difference in the top and bottom of almost anything: learning to master the basics! What are the basics of good Sunday School teaching? What are the qualities that should mark our leadership in Christian education? What ought we to strive for in our pursuit of excellence?

There are seven qualities, or characteristics, that I think every Sunday School worker ought to have.

Let Them See One

The other day I read about a man who was caught in the act of committing a crime. When the man appeared in court, the judge asked him if he needed a lawyer. He answered by saying that what he needed most was not a lawyer but a good witness. A lawyer could argue the fine points of the law, but a witness could tell from experience what happened.

The first essential of a good teacher is a personal experience with the Lord Jesus followed by a daily walk with God. The most effective Bible teaching flows out of what we are as much as what we know and how we say it. If teachers can communicate to their classes the fact that they know God in personal experience and walk with Him on a daily basis, they will be communicating the basic message of the Bible.

What people need most of all is to see Christ in the lives of others. When Mahatma Gandhi, the great Hindu leader of the Indian people, was a student in South Africa, he often attended church. He even read the New Testament through several times and was greatly impressed by it. But Gandhi never became a Christian. Listen to what Gandhi said about those churches he attended. "I got the impression that they were just a group of worldly-minded people going to church for recreation and conformity to custom. I have the highest admiration for the Christian life and for the Christ of the Bible. And I might have become a Christian if I could have seen one."

We teach by our lives as well as our words. Whatever else we do, we must give people a demonstration of the Christian life.

Cut a Straight Line

The second requirement of a good teacher is to make thorough preparation. It takes more than a baptismal certificate to be a good Sunday School teacher.

The apostle Paul admonished Timothy, "Study to shew thyself approved unto God, a workman that needeth not to be ashamed, rightly dividing the word of truth" (2 Tim. 2:15). The Greek word translated "dividing" literally means "to cut a straight line" or "to plow a straight furrow." Paul was urging Timothy to prepare well so that he would be able to lay the Word of God open in such a way that people could easily understand it and receive it.

That takes hard work. Anyone who thinks otherwise has never tried it. So to be an effective teacher, you need to start early in the week. You need to let the Word of God soak into your mind and permeate your very life. You need to attend faithfully the teacher-preparation time in your church. If you feel, as some do, that you don't need teacher-preparation time, then you virtually disqualify yourself as a teacher. An unteachable teacher can never be as effective as she should be.

Somebody has said, "The person who teaches, learns twice." That's right. They learn when they prepare, and they learn when they share. So prepare well.

Don't Be a No-Show

Third, be faithful in your attendance. Reliability and dependability are as important as capability if you are going to be an effective teacher. No matter how educated or how dedicated you may be, you can't teach effectively if you aren't present.

People sometimes excuse themselves from taking teaching positions in the church by saying, "I don't want to be tied down." When they say that to me, I remind them that Jesus was "nailed down" for them. We ought to be willing to be tied down in service for the One who was nailed down for our salvation.

Keep the Goal in Mind

Fourth, make your teaching relevant. The goal of Christian education is not just to increase Bible knowledge but to change lives.

The apostle Paul spoke of people who were "Ever learning, and never able to come to the knowledge of the truth" (2 Tim. 3:7). What a tragedy! But that is still happening today. I know of people who go to Bible conference after Bible conference; they listen to religious tapes without end, and they carry a Bible as big as a Houston telephone directory, but they are still the fussiest, crankiest, and most critical people I know.

Bible study and Bible knowledge that does not change a person's life worries me. It is a shallow and inadequate Bible teaching that does not show itself in the lives of those who study it.

The Bible is the most relevant and the most powerful Book in the world. When it is taught plainly, related practically, and received genuinely, people's lives will be transformed.

Persistent Outreach

Fifth, we need to be persistent in our outreach.

My own life is a testimony to the value of this. I grew up in a family that could best be classified as "civilized pagans." We lived within the shadow of two churches, but we never went to either of them. My family was poor and uneducated, and we felt that we did not fit in those big churches. The churches never bothered us, and we never bothered them.

Not once in my formative years, except when we went back to the country to visit my grandparents, did my family ever take me to church. When I was about fourteen years of age, a school classmate became interested in my spiritual life. He regularly attended the First Baptist Church of Port Arthur which was located about a half block from our apartment, so when his parents brought him to Sunday School, my classmate walked over to my apartment and tried to get me to go to Sunday School with him. If I was up, Mother would make me get dressed and go. If I was asleep, she left me alone. I spent some of the most miserable hours of my life staying in bed and trying to pretend that I was asleep past 9:30 on Sunday morning, so I wouldn't have to go to Sunday School.

But my friend Paul Smith persisted in coming. And in time I began attending Sunday School regularly. I learned in Sunday School that the church had a softball team and a basketball team, and if I would attend regularly I could play on those teams. I didn't know God, and I didn't care anything about Him. But I sure did know sports, and I cared about them. I was willing to take Bible study in order to play on the ball team.

The end result was that before long I became a Christian. My whole life was changed, not because a preacher came after me but because a friend and a Sunday School member persisted in outreach. I'm persuaded that if we are going to reach most of our world for Christ today, we will have to use the same kind of persistency.

Evangelistic and outreach visitation is never easy. One of the first obstacles you will encounter is indifference on the part of the people you are visiting. They will be lost or backslidden and won't seem to care. You will be tempted to say, "If they don't care about themselves, why should I care about them?"

But we must not be indifferent to other people's indifference. We must care about them even when they do not care about themselves. If Paul Smith had waited until I cared about myself before he starting caring about me, he would probably still be waiting. But Paul Smith cared about me when I didn't care about myself. In fact, it was because he cared about me that I began to care.

We can never build a different world with an indifferent church. When the concern on the inside of the church exceeds the indifference on the outside of the church, a great harvest day will come in the world. Until then we will continue to lose ground numerically and spiritually.

We make a mistake if we assume that because a person is not interested in Christ and His church today he won't be interested tomorrow. Tomorrow he may learn that his wife has cancer. Tomorrow his child may be busted for drugs. Tomorrow he may be fired from his job. Any number of things can happen that will awaken a new interest in spiritual things. So don't ever drop people from your roll or give up on them as prospects. I keep believing there must be another fourteen-year-old boy out there somewhere who is lost and could be reached if somebody would just go after him and never give up.

It is as much the duty of a teacher to train witnesses as it is to be a witness. If you have twenty members in your Sunday School class and two of them are lost, it is not only your duty to win those two to Christ, it is just as much your duty to train the other eighteen to be soul-winners.

Winning the lost is addition. Training witnesses is multiplication. Spurgeon said, "He who wins a soul draws water from a well, but he who trains a soul-winner digs a well from which thousands may drink to eternal life."

Nothing produces more results for Christ than a personal, systematic, and continuous visitation program.

A Caring and Sharing Ministry

Six, maintain a loving ministry during the week. The New Testament church was a "caring" and a "sharing" fellowship. The best way to develop and maintain such a fellowship today is through the small Sunday School class unit on an age-group basis. Teachers need to visit their class members as well as the lost.

You cannot effectively teach people you do not know. And you can't get to know people simply by being with them in a forty-five-minute classroom session on Sunday morning. But through visitation and ministry, you can gain a knowledge of people and develop a relationship with them that enhances your teaching considerably.

John Bisagno, pastor of First Baptist Church, Houston, Texas, told me that people often ask him how he is able to pastor a church with sixteen thousand members. He answers them, "I have hundreds of associate pastors called Sunday School teachers, and each one of them is in charge of a small class of fifteen to twenty people. They know each member individually, pray for them daily, visit them in their homes regularly, and minister to them personally. That's the only way I can do it."

Each Sunday School teacher needs to see himself or herself as an associate to and an extension of the pastor to carry on a loving ministry in the class.

Remember Whose Class It Is

Seven, keep a cooperative spirit. Sunday School workers can become terribly possessive and selfish of their classrooms and class rolls. I remind you that the classroom you meet in belongs to the church. The literature you use is bought by the church. Your class roll comes from the membership of the church. And you were chosen by the church to be a teacher. So your class belongs to the church. If your class needs to be divided, if your members need to promote, and if you need to meet in another room, then be cooperative and yield to what is best for the Sunday School as a whole.

In 1858 a Sunday School teacher named Kimbell walked into a shoe store in Boston and won a young shoe clerk to faith in Jesus Christ. His name was D. L. Moody. In time, D. L. Moody became one of the greatest evangelists in American history.

In his far-reaching ministry, Moody traveled to England where he awakened evangelistic zeal in the heart of a young pastor named F. B. Meyer.

F. B. Meyer became one of the great Bible expositors of all times. Eventually his ministry brought him to the United States to preach on college campuses.

In one of Meyer's crusades a student named J. Wilbur Chapman was converted to faith in Christ.

J. Wilbur Chapman became a great preacher and carried on an effective work through the YMCA. In his work, Chapman employed the services of an ex-baseball player named Billy Sunday as his assistant.

In time Billy Sunday became one of America's foremost evangelists. As a result of a crusade Sunday preached in Charlotte, North Carolina, the men of that area were so stirred spiritually that they planned a similar crusade in the city the following year.

Mordecai Ham was invited to be the evangelist for that meeting. One night during the revival meeting a tall, lanky teenage boy named Billy Graham walked down the aisle and gave his life to Christ.

Only eternity will reveal the tremendous impact of a Sunday School teacher named Kimbell who won a young man to Jesus Christ and then taught him the Word of God.

This kind of down-to-earth religious education is one of the keys to growing an evangelistic church.

13
Don't Throw in the Towel

Dr. W. A. Criswell, pastor of the First Baptist Church, Dallas, Texas, once prayed, "Oh, God, may I be in the harvest when the sun goes down."

I think all Kingdom workers start out with that desire in their hearts and that prayer on their lips. But many do not make it until sunset. They become discouraged and drop out long before quitting time.

Paul addressed this problem when he wrote, "Let us not be weary in well-doing: for in due season we shall reap, if we faint not" (Gal. 6:9). Every Christian worker must contend with the weariness that Paul talked about. It is never easy to work with volunteer help or to operate on freewill offerings. It is always taxing to try to arouse a sleeping church or to turn an indifferent world to God. It is a draining responsibility to deal with immature saints and to contend with Satan at the same time.

And not all fields give the same yield. Some Christian workers have to work in the most discouraging of circumstances. They are forced to labor with dead congregations that meet in dilapidated buildings located in declining neighborhoods, in depressed cities. When that's the case, it is hard to keep going.

It may be that you are in one of those hard places and barren times now, and you are thinking about giving up, throwing in the towel, and quitting. We all feel that way at times.

But don't do it! Don't quit. To grow an evangelistic church

takes time. And we often have to stay through hard and discouraging circumstances. The devil does not bother people or
churches who are asleep on the job. But when we undertake a
great work for the Lord, the devil tries to defeat us by either
outside opposition or inward discouragement.

This kind of discouragement and the desire to quit are not
new. They lie behind the words of the apostle Paul to Titus
when he wrote, "For this cause left I thee in Crete, that thou
shouldest set in order the things that are wanting, and ordain
elders in every city, as I had appointed thee" (Titus 1:5).

The Book of Titus has been called a letter to a discouraged
pastor. Paul had sent Titus to Crete on a special assignment to
strengthen the churches. But the work in Crete was hard, and
the people were difficult, if not impossible, to work with. One
of their own poets, Epimenides, had said that all Cretans were
liars, that they were wicked brutes and lazy gluttons (Titus
1:12). And the apostle Paul agreed with this assessment.

Even though Titus was a tough preacher, he had grown
weary and discouraged in Crete and wanted to quit. Some
people think that Titus had written to Paul requesting a new
assignment to an easier place.

But Paul refused the request and wrote back these words to
Titus. He told Titus that the reasons why he wanted to quit
were the very reasons why he was assigned to Crete in the first
place. Crete was a hard place, but God needed a good man
there. Paul's advice to Titus was to stay in Crete and to do the
work God had placed him there to do.

What or where is your Crete? Of course, geographically,
Crete is an island in the Mediterranean Sea. But it is representative of any place or any thing that you would like to get away
from. It represents a hard place, a difficult situation, or an
impossible people. It may be a place of suffering, opposition, or
sorrow. We all have our Cretes, no matter who we are.

Why did God put Titus in Crete? Why did Paul encourage

him to stay in that hard place and not to quit? Why does God leave us in the tough places, the hard spots, the discouraging situations of life? Why doesn't He get us out and move us on?

There are three reasons why God left Titus in Crete and why He often chooses to leave us in our Crete: (1) He leaves us in Crete because He loves Crete. (2) He leaves us in Crete to develop us. And (3) He leaves us in Crete so we can be His instruments in redemption.

God Loves Crete

There were no people in the ancient world who had a worse reputation than the people of Crete. The very name *Crete* was synonymous with dishonesty, overindulgence, intemperance, and laziness (Titus 1:12). But in spite of all of that, God loved Crete and wanted to redeem it. That's why he left Titus there.

If ever there was a place and a people that you would think would be beyond God's love and concern, surely it would have been Crete. But the very presence of Titus there tells us that Crete mattered to God.

There are no people so bad and no situations so hopeless that God does not care about them. God loves the whole world, and Crete is a vital part of it.

How could God love a place as wicked as Crete? In her book *One in Seven,* Margaret Slattery tells of a young couple who visited the Bay of Fundy in Nova Scotia, and, standing on the gorge, witnessed the awesome sight of the fifty-foot tide, the highest in the world, come swirling in. Watching the water pushing, pouring, pounding in through the Bore, over the low flats, over the banks, and over the boulders, they were left breathless.

When the majestic display of power had spent its force, the girl said quietly, "Why should the personal affairs of two people like us claim even for a moment the attention of a God of might and majesty like that?"

"Because He is God," responded her companion.

Why does God love Crete? It is not because Cretans are lovable; it is because He is love. God loved Crete not because of what it was, but because of what He is. His love is not dependent upon our character but upon His character.

Love is the supreme and dominant attribute of God. Paul declared, "God commendeth his love toward us, in that, while we were yet sinners, Christ died for us" (Rom. 5:8). God loves us not in our goodness, nor in our purity, nor in our righteousness, but in our sinfulness. And the cross of Christ is the supreme demonstration of that love.

But God's love did not begin at Calvary. Jeremiah declared, "The Lord hath appeared of old unto me, saying, Yea, I have loved thee with an everlasting love: therefore with lovingkindness have I drawn thee" (Jer. 31:3). Note that God's love is everlasting. It had no beginning, and it has no end. God loved us, so He created us in His image. God loved us, so He gave us freedom of choice. God loved us, so He sought Adam in the garden. God loved us, and thus He gave us His law. And, finally and ultimately, God loved us and sent His Son to be our Redeemer.

That love of God is expressed to us in twenty-five familiar and beautiful words, "For God so loved the world, that he gave his only begotten Son, that whosoever believeth in him should not perish, but have everlasting life" (John 3:16).

The love of God is immeasurable, unmistakable, and unending. It reaches wherever people are. The last stanza of "The Love of God" was supposedly found written on the wall of a hospital:

> Could we with ink the ocean fill,
>   And were the skies of parchment made,
> Were every blade of grass a quill,
>   And every man a scribe by trade,

> To write the love of God above,
> Would drain the ocean dry,
> Nor could the scroll contain the whole,
> Though stretched from sky to sky.

That's the love of God. So, Christian worker, don't quit! Don't give up on Crete until God does. God loves that hard place where you are, and that's why He put you there.

God Cares About You

God left Titus in Crete not only because He cared about Crete, but also because He cared about Titus. He left Titus there not in order to punish him, but to perfect him. It was not to make him miserable, but to make him mature. God's goal for our lives is not to make us comfortable, but to make us conform to the image of His Son, Jesus Christ. He is more concerned about our character than about our comfort.

God is not simply interested in saving souls; He wants to develop a Christlike character in us. Christian character is not something we inherit or something that is given to us. It is something we develop. Through life's experiences and our response to them, character is built. Troubles and hardships mixed with faith make us into the kind of people we ought to be. Character does not come cheap. It almost always involves suffering on the part of someone. When a football coach wants to build a good team, he does not send his players out on the field to play with soft pillows. The coach puts them to work against rough opponents, a buckling frame, a tackling dummy, and through strenuous exercises. God does the same thing with us. To give us the strength of steadfastness and patience in our character, He marches us at times against tough opponents, against temptation, against public opinion, and against discouragement.

Great civilizations and great people are not made in softness but in challenge and response to that challenge. Great ministers are made the same way.

The apostle Paul learned humility and faith through the things he suffered (2 Cor. 12:9). Even our Lord Jesus was perfected through suffering (Heb. 2:10). He was made complete through His experiences that He might better minister to us. And it took Calvary to do it.

So the Lord often allows us to go through painful experiences and endure hardships because these are the things that develop us into the kind of people we need to be. God allows some suffering and some difficulties because there are some things to be accomplished in our character that can be brought about only by suffering and trials (1 Pet. 1:7).

Great men and women are born out of hardship. If one reads enough biographies, one will get to thinking that there can't be great people except that they suffer greatly.

God knows that one can't develop strong men and women in easy places. People who have never had their faith tested don't know whether they have faith. God wants to make you and me like Christ, and He allows us to stay in hard places to make us better.

James tells us we should be happy when different kinds of trials and troubles come our way because these are the means of developing in us the strength of character that is a necessary part of Christian maturity (Jas. 1:2-4). Pressures produce patience, and patience leads to perfection. As carbon under the tremendous pressure of tons of earth produces a beautiful diamond, so God allows our character to be formed under the pressure of our circumstances.

Some unknown poet has put it this way:

> When God wants to drill a man
> And thrill a man,
> And skill a man,

When God wants to mold a man
To play the noblest part;
When He yearns with all His heart,
To create so great and bold a man,
That all the world shall be amazed,
Watch His methods, watch His ways!
How He ruthlessly perfects,
Whom He royally elects!
How He hammers him and hurts him,
And with mighty blows converts him
Into trial shapes of clay which
Only God understands;
While his tortured heart is crying
And he lifts beseeching hands!
How He bends but never breaks,
When His good He undertakes;
How He uses whom He chooses,
And with every purpose fuses him;
By every act induces him
To try his splendor out -
God knows what He's about!

I have lived long enough to thank God for my trials and my troubles. What I thought at one time was the benediction to my ministry turned out to be the invocation. What seemed to me to be the worst thing that could happen to me has turned out to be the best thing.

So don't quit, fellow worker! God is making you into the kind of person He wants you to be. And He may be preparing you for greater usefulness in His kingdom. Don't give up on that discouraging situation. It oftentimes takes a hard place and difficult people to make us into the kind of persons God wants us to be.

God Wants to Use Us

Finally, God left Titus in Crete because He wanted to use Titus as an instrument to change the world. Paul told Titus that he was left in Crete to "set in order" things that were wanting (1:5). The term *set in order* is a medical term that means "to set in joint." It describes what a doctor does when you go to him with a broken bone. Because the parts of the bone are out of right relationship with one another, the doctor must pull them back into place, so they can heal properly, and the limb can be useful once again. Though setting a bone back in place is very painful and unpleasant, it is a necessary part of healing.

That's a part of what God has called us to do. When I open the doors of our church, it is like opening the doors of a hospital emergency room. The wounded, the hurting, the bruised and bleeding come in a steady flow. And I am glad they do. It is a part of my calling to help them put their broken, shattered lives back together again. It is a part of your calling also.

It is difficult and sometimes unpleasant work, but God has called us to do it, and we must be faithful.

The people of Crete were out of joint with God and out of joint with one another. God sent Titus there to be a spiritual orthopedist. He was not sent there for his comfort and ease. He was not sent there for his own professional advancement. He was sent there to set things in order in the churches.

Crete could never be right until the church was right. And the church could never be right until the preacher was right. By the same token our world will never be right until the church is right, and the church will never be right until preachers are right. So, pastor, don't quit! Don't resign! Stay where you are as long as God leaves you there and set things in order. Do what God put you there to do and stay everlastingly at it until Jesus comes again.

We are the body of Christ. Once our Lord incarnated Himself for thirty-three years in the human body. Now He perpetually incarnates Himself in His new body: the church. Through His living spirit, He dwells in every believer, and thus we become His body on earth. The Holy Spirit does not haunt houses. He does not jump out of the Bible and grab people. He dwells in us. The Holy Spirit uses people to do His work. I don't know of anyone who has ever been converted to Christ since the time of Christ without some other human instrumentality being involved. You say, "Well, what about a man who is converted by reading a Gideon Bible in a hotel room?" Who put the Bible there? Who paid for it? Who printed it? You ask, "What about the apostle Paul?" He had the witness of Stephen and others. Plus, Ananias came to Paul and instructed him in the ways of the Lord. And as a Pharisee, Paul had memorized scores of passages from the Old Testament.

The short of the matter is that God uses people to reach other people. We are His instruments in world redemption. God could have used angels, but we are better than the angels, for they know nothing of forgiveness and grace.

We must not pray that God will take us out of the world, out of the difficult situations. We must pray that God will leave us here, so we can be His instruments in redeeming the world.

It was a supreme compliment to Titus that God should put him in Crete. A hard place needs a tough preacher. Anyone can handle the easy places. God oftens sends His best workers to the worst of spots. Take that hard place you are in as a challenge and a compliment, match it with commitment, and God will bless you.

Knute Rockne, the great Notre Dame football coach, used to say, "When the going gets tough, the tough get going." That's my challenge to you. Life is tough, and if you sail its seas long enough, you will run into a storm. When you do, don't jump ship. Don't ask to be discharged. Don't throw in the

towel. Pray rather for the strength to stay at your post and
fulfill your duty.

Someone has penned these lines that ought to express the
desire of every hurting, discouraged pastor's heart:

Give me a love that leads the way,
    A faith that nothing can dismay,
    A hope no disappointments tire,
    A passion that will burn like fire,
    Let me not sink to be a clod:
    Make me thy tool, oh, flame of God.